JOURNEYS
TO
MOTHER
LOVE

JOURNEYS TO MOTHER LOVE

NINE WOMEN TELL THEIR STORIES OF
FORGIVENESS AND HEALING

COMPILED BY
Catherine Lawton

CLADACH
Publishing

JOURNEYS TO MOTHER LOVE
Nine Women Tell their Stories of Forgiveness & Healing
© 2012 by CLADACH Publishing
Greeley, Colorado 80633
www.cladach.com

Scripture quotations, unless otherwise indicated, are taken from THE HOLY
BIBLE, NEW INTERNATIONAL VERSION®, NIV® Copyright ©1973,
1978, 1984, 2011 by Biblica, Inc.™ Used by permission. All rights reserved world-
wide.
Scripture quotations marked NRSV are taken from the New Revised Standard Ver-
sion Bible, Copyright © 1989, Division of Christian Education of the National
Council of the Churches of Christ in the United States of America. Used by
permission. All rights reserved.
Scripture quotations marked AMPLIFIED are taken from the Amplified® Bible,
Copyright © 1954, 1958, 1962, 1964, 1965, 1987 by The Lockman Foundation
Used by permission." (www.Lockman.org)
Scripture quotations marked NLT are taken from the Holy Bible, New Living
Translation, copyright 1996. Used by permission of Tyndale House Publishers, Inc.,
Wheaton, Illinois 60189. All rights reserved.
Scripture quotations marked KJV are taken from the King James Version Bible.

"Finding the Blessings in Alzheimer's" is excerpted from *Life Lessons from a Baker's
Dozen: 1 Mother, 13 Children, and their Journey to Peace with Alzheimer's* by Kerry
Luksic, www.kerryluksic.com. Used by permission.

Library of Congress Cataloging-in-Publication Data
Journeys to mother love : nine women tell their stories of forgiveness & healing /
compiled by Catherine Lawton.
     p. cm.
Includes bibliographical references and index.
ISBN 978-0-9818929-5-5 (alk. paper)
ISBN 0-9818929-5-7 (alk. paper)
1. Mother and child—Religious aspects—Christianity.
2. Motherhood—Religious aspects—Christianity. 3. Motherhood—Literary col-
lections. I. Lawton, Catherine.
BV4529.18.J68 2012
248.8'431--dc23
2012027230

"Each mother-child relationship teaches us our
limitations and our strengths. It changes us in
constantly unfolding ways and entwines us in the
unpredictable mystery of another life."

~ Caroline Kennedy

"Surely I have calmed and quieted my soul, like a
weaned child with its mother."

~ Psalm 131:2

CONTENTS

INTRODUCTION

Many writers have said that mother love is one of the strongest of instincts. What is "mother love"? For me it was a baptism that washed over me and flooded my heart when I first held my newborn baby in my arms. I fed that child when she was hungry, washed her, clothed her, rocked her, protected her, trained her, enfolded her, carried her, prepared her, and released her. And while I identify with the words of the Irish poet, "Lord, thou art hard on mothers: We suffer in their coming and in their going,"[1] I believe that mother love seldom dwells on the pain or counts the cost. Instead, this caring, nurturing, self-sacrificing force "protects, trusts, hopes, perseveres"[2] on behalf of this miracle of life, this product of our own body, this heaven-sent mystery of a helpless suckling developing into independent womanhood in her own right.

Sadly, along the way, many obstacles may arise to block the effective expression of mother love. "Although most mothers instinctively love their children, learning to properly nurture them is a process," wrote Grace Ketterman.[3] Mother love doesn't always come easy; it isn't always expressed in ways that are healthy; and though the mother may feel it, a child can't always receive it.

We—the writers of this book—represent four different generations and come from various backgrounds and places. What we have in common is this: We are all mothers and we all have mothers (whether or not they are still living). For each of us, coming to the place of freely receiving and giving love in the mother-child relationship has been a sometimes difficult journey.

For example, one woman felt all her life the impact of being the lesser-loved sibling, until finally after many years she found it in her heart to be thankful for both her favored brother and her mother. Another young woman had difficulty showing love to her little children until she was healed of the memories of an earlier abortion, and until she forgave herself and experienced a heart connection with the aborted baby. A third woman was distanced from her mother because of her fear of being like her, until the Lord gave her a new heart to see her mother in new light and to serve her in new ways. More than one story touches on the concept of generational patterns that needed to be broken in order to allow a new way of mother-child relating.

In sharing these personal memoirs, which are testimonies of God's grace, we have tried not to offer pat answers. We simply and openly tell our stories in hopes that many readers—mothers and daughters like us—will be helped. We believe the power of prayer, the Word of God, the working of the Holy Spirit and the body of Christ are transforming every area of our lives. So we offer hope and tell what helped us, and what may renew your relationships as well.

Mothers (and fathers) aren't perfect; they all make mistakes. They were parented imperfectly and they have parented us imperfectly. But we will go through our entire lives being the child of our parents.

The Lord with whom a thousand years is as a day, who created us and thoroughly knows us, in his infinite wisdom and foreknowledge has designed us in such a way that we continue to carry within us the child we were. What do we do, then, with this inner child, who is forever part of us? What about the times she cries, feels neglected, or forsaken, or fearful ... when her emotional needs have not been met in healthy ways?

Francis and Judith MacNutt, of Christian Healing Ministries, state, "Unfortunately, in our fallen humanity, there are no perfect parents. Subsequently, many people carry wounds or voids they incurred early in life from one or both of their parents, such as unmet needs, absence, neglect, harsh words, or abusive behavior ... Nevertheless, through the power of the Holy Spirit, the Lord can go back and fill in any of those wounds with his perfect love."[4]

Like all other parts of our selves, we bring that inner child to Jesus. We let Jesus love that child. His presence begins a process, an unfolding of forgiveness, peace, thankfulness, prayerfulness, a renewed mind, right thinking, and right relatedness. We begin to experience the "joyful wholeness"[5] God has for us in all our relationships. Specifically, in this book we are focusing on mother-child relationships. And every woman is a daughter and/or a mother.

In these nine stories the reader will find stages in the mother-child relationship healing process:

- Acknowledge that the child within is hurting
- Allow Jesus into the picture
- Receive "new eyes" to see that your mother (and father) also had within her a hurting child
- Make choices to forgive your mother and to be renewed in your own mothering
- Experience new appreciation for your mother (and/or father, child, sibling)
- Enjoy fellowship with your mother (and/or father, child, sibling)

Much has been written about "father wounds." But our mothers are in many ways the ground of our beings. "Mother is the home we come from. She is nature, soil, ocean," said psychologist Erich Fromm.[6] Mother love goes deep; and mother wounds go deep.

God has described his own nurturing character in terms of a mother's love for her children:

"As a mother comforts her child, so I will comfort you" (Isaiah 66:13a, NRSV).

"Can a mother forget the baby at her breast and have no compassion on the child she has borne? Though she may forget, I will not forget you!" (Isaiah 49:15).

"I led them with cords of human kindness, with ties of love. To them I was like one who lifts a little child to the cheek, and I bent down to feed them" (Hosea 11:4).

"He will cover you with his feathers, and under his wings you will find refuge" (Psalm 91:4a).

"He shielded him and cared for him; he guarded him as the apple of his eye, like an eagle that stirs up its nest and hovers over its young, that spreads its wings to catch them and carries them aloft ... [But] You deserted the Rock, who fathered you; you forgot the God who gave you birth" (Deuteronomy 32:10b-11 & 18).

And Jesus, when he walked on earth, said:

"How often I have longed to gather your children together, as a hen gathers her chicks under her wings...." (Luke 13:34).

About this verse John Stott writes, "[Jesus] was clearly and deliberately developing a feminine image of God.... Although this does not give us liberty to address God as 'our mother,' since he invariably reveals himself as our 'father,' and Jesus told us to approach him thus, nevertheless it obliges us to remember that our Father-God has motherly qualities."[6]

God instituted motherhood and created the powerful force of "mother love." Because his own nurturing, protective, life-giving love for us is exemplified in the love of a mother for her child, the Lord is working in our mother-child relationships to make them a more true representation, a clearer picture of his love. He makes a way for us to experience deep healing, even—as the experiences of these nine women illustrate—when death, disease, disobedience, or distance has separated us from our mothers.

God's love—often made tangible in mother love—is that strong!

- Catherine Lawton, June 2012
Greeley, Colorado

1. From "The Mother" by Padraig Pearse, in *A Little Book of Irish Verse* (Belfast: Appletree Press, 1991), p. 51.

2. 1 Corinthians 13:7

3. Grace Ketterman, *Call Me Blessed: Becoming a Mother of Honor* (Kansas City: Beacon Hill Press), 1997, p. 3.

4. http://christianhealingmin.net/prayer-ministry14/sample-prayers/291-a-mothers-blessing

5. "Joyful wholeness" is how my pastor, Doug Brown, aptly describes this sanctifying work and state of grace.

6. Erich Fromm, *The Art of Loving*, (Harper & Row, 1956, HarperCollins, 1984, Harper Perennial Modern Classic, 2006), p. 38.

7. John Stott, *The Birds Our Teachers* (Grand Rapids: Baker Books, 2001), p. 73.

1
RUN, RUN AS FAST AS YOU CAN
by A.R. Cecil

"My peace I give you."
-John 14:27

The small town of my youth is tucked away in the middle of the state of Kentucky. It was a good, safe place for children to grow up in the 1950s. My siblings and I knew every street, explored most. We could be seen canvassing the town, barefoot in the summer and pulling a sled behind us in the winter. This unbridled independence freed up our mother from the need to learn to drive. My father would take my brother, two sisters, and me to school in the mornings. We were on our own to find a way home unless it rained, in which case my father would leave the five-and-dime store he co-owned with my aunt and come and get us.

Sunny days must have consistently won over rainy ones because most of my memories are rooted in the long treks after the three o'clock dismissal. I would hightail it home, making every shortcut possible through all the backyards that stood between the elementary school and my front door.

"Run, run as fast as you can," I would tell my feet, as I was distancing myself from those immature children who picked favorites and then picked on those they had deemed inferior.

There was no doubt whether or not I was on the list of the popular kids, but I never was ridiculed. I had made myself invisible, an ability that was fostered in me by the dynamics in my home. This skill was utilized in almost every social circle. Go to school, do a little work; come home and see how my mother was doing; that routine suited me very well until it dawned on me that I could not remain invisible forever and survive.

One day a child, the next we step out of that state and forever close the magical door that separates our innocence from reality. But, in many regards, I was never a child, not really. I was always my mother's keeper with my hand on her pulse: "Mom is sad today"; "Mom isn't feeling well again"; "Mom must have worked too hard."

The realization that I had to find a way for myself in life occurred toward the end of those eight years of grade school on a day in late April. Was it the sudden downpour? No matter the reason, the unexpected change in the weather that April day brought me to the conclusion that I needed a plan for my life. The bright blue sky at dismissal turned black and then proceeded to release every drop of its accumulated precipitation. My father's plan for picking us up from school did not include sudden downpours.

"Run, run as fast as you can," I told my feet. "Run to get out of the rain."

I ran until the need to catch my breath made running impossible. I had made it as far as the abandoned lot, the last unclaimed plot in the subdivision. Then I stopped. Soon, though, I journeyed on and finally entered the house drenched and chilled to the bone. The muted sounds of organ music from the soap opera in the next room greeted me. I imagined a drama being played out in my life:

Drenched, unimportant girl finds meaning in life by meeting a movie star while standing in the abandoned lot on the corner of West Virginia Avenue and Doctor Street. He was riding by and saw in her a great undiscovered beauty. He could see beyond the plain features and the shapeless figure in the school uniform and cardigan to see a prize of great value. He got out of his limousine and went down on one knee in the rain at which point he vowed to love her forever. Singers came out of nowhere, dancing in the rain as they twirled brightly-colored umbrellas, all in perfect, synchronized steps. Then the rain stopped and a rainbow arched over the production which served as a backdrop for the finale. The sweet-spirited girl flung off her cardigan and navy blue skirt which turned out to be a wraparound one. Underneath was a golden gown with spaghetti straps. She began to dance with her newfound love. When the music ended applause went up where houses used to stand. The entire street had been transformed into a theater where ten thousand admiring spectators stood begging for an encore.

The applause at the end of the commercial for Chrysler's sleek new car broke in and ended my daydream. Through it all—the soaps and interspersed commercials—my mother slept. She would doze on the daybed set up for her naps while the soap operas ever so slowly told the sordid intermeshing of the lives of many beautiful people. I stopped in the bathroom and rubbed my hair with a towel to get the majority of the water out of it. An unintentional glance in the mirror shattered any hopes that a movie star would ever propose to me. I dropped my wet clothing on the floor and pulled on a casual outfit which included my favorite sweatshirt. In it, I felt secure. Then I slid onto the couch that sat adjacent to my mother's bed. I felt so far from being a beautiful person, and I did not have the rain to blame. I was not a beautiful person, would probably never be one. If I was a beautiful person, I would not have been invisible. The innate gift of deductive reasoning, unfortunately, kept all of my fantasies from having much of a shelf life.

My mother might not have watched much of the long and drawn out misery of the characters in the soaps, but I did. A month's worth of episodes could have been missed and the story would not have skipped a beat (though I never had the opportunity to test that theory). While I sat there on that particular day, I pictured my life and concluded it would be very different than the lives of the people in the soap operas. I might not marry a movie star and be the great beauty on his arm, but I could be a good person. The ugly duckling would probably never become a swan; the ability to influence with my personality was never going to happen; but good might be obtainable. With enough work, that is. My newly-acquired status as a teenager was the dawn of reality that erased any childish notion of life always being good and love automatically given. I would need to work.

"Earn, earn my way into the hearts of others! That's the way it works!" became my battle cry.

Then the emotion of anger rose up in me. It too was new, the unfortunate companion of awareness. Only a resolve to someday live differently eased the pain and gave me hope. When everyone was sleeping and tears rolled down the sides of my face, I would pray in the dark, "Jesus, help me be a good person and have a good life. Amen."

I felt that my father worked hard to provide a good life. He was a good man, a respected merchant in our small town. Since Mother didn't drive, he was in charge of getting the groceries. Every day, six days a week, he went to Mr. Polin's grocery across the street from his store, called my mother on the phone, and wrote down the list: "Bread, eggs, roast beef, chicken noodle soup ... how many cans?" Then he'd shop and come home to a late lunch. On occasion I was sent to town with the list. "Keep the kid busy" must have been the reason that replaced a two-minute phone call with a fifteen-minute walk. Up one long hill and down the backside of it, around the courthouse, and there was my father's store. We children, whose father owned the store, were allowed to visit the candy case just inside the entrance, pick any piece we liked, and not pay one red cent. I usually picked a large, jellied orange slice with sugar sprinkles; I had convinced myself it was fruit, not candy, and, therefore, a very acceptable snack.

At the grocer's, I trailed behind my father, as we went down one long aisle, made the turn at the end, and came back up the other long aisle. I never asked for Cokes or cookies; our family budget would not have permitted such luxuries. I just trailed along, examining the way in which the produce was stacked and wondering: *If I remove one of the bottom apples, will all of them come rolling down?* We'd end up at the cash register where Dad and Mr. Polin would talk about the weather and if it was too early to put the tomatoes in the ground, or how big they were getting. Here they were, two men who served side by side in the battle of Anzio, talking about the weather and tomatoes. In recent years, I have learned my father saw unbelievable atrocities while overseas and came back a different man than the husband of four months, who left when Pearl Harbor became his call to bear arms. He never spoke of the war, but its effect must have been what was written in his eyes. There was a far-off look that I noticed when he thought no one was looking. Was the look in his eyes a result of what he left behind on the front or what he returned to find?

In my mother's heart were sorrows he could not have understood. My parents belonged to a generation that did not talk about their feelings. So, my father did what he could and lived by reading seed catalogues in the winter and planting tomatoes in the spring. My part was to simply trail along, not asking any questions or breaking into wherever his thoughts had taken him. As I was my mother's companion for TV's "Guiding Light," I was my father's silent confidante, ever ready to pour out words of encouragement and comfort whenever he chose to turn and acknowledge me. If he ever had, I would have told him, "I know you work really hard and you don't have time for fun, but I just want you to know how much I love you." Instead, all I could do was trail along behind him and keep myself from removing the apple from the bottom of the stack. Instinctively, I knew my role in life was to be good. How could I possibly add to my mother's or father's pain?

However, within that quiet little girl with no apparent needs lived a person with a great imagination. In that shell, I lived and grew and planned until there emerged a way to pull all the loose threads of my life together. I'd be a good mother the way my father's mother had been. I never met this grandmother; she died two months before I was born. But, she must have been perfect in every way. Words were never used to share her with the grandchildren. I came to believe that to speak of her would break into a memory so precious that the interpretations of others might distort it. Therefore, I formed my own conclusions regarding her, based on the bits and pieces of her life's work. There were pillowcases and napkins with detailed stitching and a child's coat with smocking across the front. A Vermeer painting of a young girl bending low over her sewing in a dim light supplied the needed flesh and face to the one who must have sewed late into the night while her six children slept. Also, she left furniture that could have only belonged in the home of a truly caring and loving person. A corner cabinet of the finest quality, a spool bed, and a mahogany dining room table, all having seen many coats of wax, spoke of a home where only good memories must have been made. My father would see his mother in me. I would be the best imaginable mother and my children would hold me up in high esteem. "Our mother is perfect; she is such a dear," was the way this part of my future would play out. And when that wondrous moment came, my father would smile and say, "Yes, she is. I knew she would turn out just like my mother."

Ironically, my noble destiny to be a good mother, motivated by the life of my paternal grandmother, was a dream that I shared only with my maternal grandmother. When talking to her, though, I conveniently left out my inspiration, aware even at an early age that jealousy is a powerful emotion. In this case, it might have prejudiced Grandmother from giving me the sought-after approval. I needed someone with whom I could share my heart and I felt safe in sharing this corner because the plan was so noble. How could anyone find fault with it or try to rearrange it? Besides, Grandmother was the only available person. She lived on the backside of that hill I went up and down on my way downtown to my father's store. As a result, I frequently dropped in. Most of the visits were so mundane that I have only fleeting glimpses of them in my memory. "Would you please get the bowl down from the top shelf before you go?" was one. Another memory was cookies served on a faded china plate. ("If you want a cookie," my sister would say, "go visit Grandmother.") But the main impression I took away from my visits was not the one made on my taste buds but on my back. In Grandmother's house, I felt the need to sit still and straight while we engaged in small talk that should have been reserved for two strangers on a park bench. (*Are a couple of cookies worth all this discomfort?* I'd ask myself.)

By the age of fifteen, I had fine-tuned the details of my

plan. I'd marry a farmer and we would have six sons. Life on the farm would be idyllic. I could can tomatoes and beans in the late summer and quilt in the winter. The six sons could help their father on the farm. Since the small town of my childhood was surrounded by farmland in every direction for twenty to thirty miles, I'd surely have no trouble in finding a farmer.

The green light to go ahead and reveal my heart to Grandmother finally came after she gave me two back-to-back compliments: one for my height and one for my hair. Only a sophomore in high school, I already stood a towering foot over her four feet, nine inches. She was as short on words as she was on inches, so her compliments went something like this:

"Be glad you can reach the top shelf of the cupboard," she said, complimenting me on my height.

"Don't do anything to your hair. It looks good like it is," she added, complimenting me on my hair.

The "anything" was in reference to the trend at the time to bleach hair. My older sister had already become a blonde, and it had upped her social status considerably. I had enough sense to know it wouldn't have upped mine a notch. I would have only looked like a tall, skinny, freckled, blonde girl instead of the tall, skinny, freckled, brown-haired girl that I was.

Grandmother had been a farmer's wife and I thought she would appreciate her granddaughter wanting to follow in her footsteps; we could bond through this mutual experience. She was a hard worker, who hit the linoleum running in the morning. And she was religious. Her faith enabled her to be strong when faced with the trials of an alcoholic husband, and a son who struggled under the same temptation. All of Grandmother's acquaintances called her "Miss Ella." The title before her name spoke of the respect she had earned as a gentle and soft-spoken warrior. Unfortunately, sharing the plans for my life on that day of the two compliments did not result in even her usual few words. She simply raised her eyebrows in such a way as to say: "Do you know how hard it is to be a farmer's wife?" Her reaction produced the sufficient amount of cold water, which doused that version of the dream. Dreams, I have learned, are only the yeast of the bread. What shape they take is not in our hands.

Four more years would go by before there was another significant encounter with Grandmother. By now she had another brown-eyed, blonde-haired granddaughter, as I finally succumbed to the trend. I was getting ready to be launched into the world and decided it was time to reinvent myself; no farmer had made his way to my door. Even though I was only going to the city sixty miles away and would be returning every weekend, I felt obligated to drop in at Grandmother's for a farewell visit. Because I had built this visit up in my mind, I was nervous and began chatting away. At first, I kept the conversation light and even funny. All that talking, however, took an unexpected, woeful turn. Out tumbled many fears with a hint of the underlying anger. Then, since I didn't like what I was hearing, I iced it over by backtracking with remarks that served only as a layer of guilt. Any hope of becoming the person in my plan fell like a house of cards as it succumbed to the puffs of hot air which punctuated my thoughts. In that moment, it became very clear why I had chosen the status of invisibility all these years; invisible people don't talk too much. One moment in the spotlight had revealed every corner of my wretched heart.

There is no hope for me, I groaned within my spirit.

All the while I was talking, Grandmother had intently listened without interrupting, like a psychologist who is

assessing her client's situation. When I finished, silence
filled the space between us and activated my brain with
excuses to move out of it. "That's OK," I could tell her.
"You don't have to respond to all that rambling." Or, I could
fake the need to go to the bathroom. Or, I could glance
at the clock and say, "Look how late it has gotten! Got to
be going."

Before I could act on one of the ideas, Grandmother
spoke and her words revealed the strength behind the small
frame.

"We must take up our cross," she simply said.

She could have told me I'd do great, that everything
would be rosy; but that was not her style. The comment
even seemed like a reprimand at the time. Little did I know
those words would be the very road to fulfilling my noble
destiny.

Grandmother lived to see me marry a fine man (though
not a farmer) and have one child (a daughter, a bright
and beautiful addition to our family). The plan, though
altered, had obviously been set in motion. I kept our home
immaculate; at every holiday, it looked like a Christmas
card. Every spring and summer the flower beds around the
house declared: "Care and love reside within." Boundless
energy undergirded the dream. As long as I worked hard
and pretended to be happy, surely the dream would eventually take flight and become reality. Maybe there would be
a day when I wouldn't have to work so hard or pretend so
much.... Then the second daughter was born.

As a newborn, the first daughter had required rocking,
but this new baby was unsettled in a way that my husband
and I sensed was beyond normal. One month after caring
for "the baby that would not settle," she was diagnosed
with cancer. Fourteen months passed and the surgery and
radiation treatments did not fulfill their intended purpose;

the cancer was back and now in her bone marrow. Chemotherapy was the new, last hope. My life began to whirl until
all the edges were lovingly blurred. When life is too big,
God will erase some of it. Go to the treatment. Go to the
grocery store. Go for more radiation. Go to the older sister's
school program. Go to the surgeon's to see when he wants
to schedule another surgery. Go to the cookout. Go in for
a finger stick to see if the baby's blood count would allow
another treatment.

"Run, run as fast as you can," I read to the sister. "You
can't catch me. I'm the gingerbread man."

Run, run as fast as I could, I could not outrun God
anymore, like I had been unable as a child to outrun the
rain. One day I simply couldn't run any more. I was on my
way to take the baby to a chemotherapy treatment when a
traffic light became the place where the running stopped.
The light had just turned red, which placed our car first in
line. The intersection filled with people. I turned to look at
the baby and she smiled at me. I smiled back, outwardly.
But my thoughts were in turmoil as I looked at my baby.

*How can you smile at me? Do you know where I am taking
you? If I could explain this to you, I would, but I can't. Will you
think your mother is unkind; will you hold this against me?*

I turned to look forward, to wait out the light.

All these people, where are they going?

They were walking fast as if they had important things
to do or interesting places to go. Some of them were even
laughing.

*How could they be laughing on a day like this? Don't they
know we are running out of hope? Run, run, run; we are
running out of hope.*

"Jesus," I prayed. "If you are real, help me believe in
you." When had I added the phrase, "If you are real"? My
prayers as a child were ones based on faith. But the prayers

had not worked; how else was I to think now? "Trust enough and all your dreams will come true," my childish heart had believed. I trusted; and look where it got me. I had given my best across the board and see what I had to show for it. *Run, run, have I been running in place all these years?*

Baby Jesus in a manger; "Silent night, holy night"; Santa coming with toys; but remember the real reason behind Christmas; Jesus dying on a cross; poor Jesus, three days in a tomb; then Easter with new dresses and candy in the shape of eggs from my father's store—these were the main events that were highlighted on every calendar of my life. Other children might have focused on their toys and candy, but I always remembered to be true to the meaning. "I was a good child, God. Is this the way you treat those who try really hard to be good children?"

"Jesus, if you are real"—? *How could he not be real? If he was just an idea, how has every generation since his life on earth kept the thought going so we'd have special events to celebrate? Logic would say that such a fabrication making it down through the centuries would be impossible. But, if he is real, how does he work? How am I to think on him?*

"Jesus, if you are real . . ." I whispered this time. I couldn't run anymore. I had run out of steam to make my dream come true. I couldn't stay invisible and silent anymore. Then I remembered that there was no dream nobler than this one. I had no other place to run. This dream needed to be fulfilled, but how?

The intersection cleared, the light turned green, and we drove on to our appointment. The magazines in the waiting room helped distract me, so I was able to keep from embarrassing myself with uncontrollable tears.

That recipe will work. I'll write in down on the back of a bank deposit. The garden in this picture is lovely. What plants did they use to create the flower bed? Mauve is a good color for a dining room. What would it take to repaint ours?

After the treatment, I took the baby home and placed the sleeping child in the middle of my big bed. The medicine they gave her for nausea, which did not work, made her sleep for now. The toddler would need constant assistance. It was only noon and I could hear my mother-in-law down in the kitchen serving lunch.

Wonder if she is fixing peanut butter and jelly or grilled cheese for the big sister?

Three more hours—I did the math. It would take at least three more hours until the baby's system would stop the violent reaction from the toxins, or there was just nothing left in her to come out. There would be twenty-three more treatments, one treatment every three weeks for one-and-a-half years. That was how long our baby would be subjected to this new, last hope. She continued to sleep, and I was grateful for this rest period. I was also grateful that the child beside me would never remember these days in the middle of my big bed. While she slept, I read. It was a book about an encounter a man had with Jesus in prayer. There was a preacher on television whose teaching made more sense than anything my husband or I had heard before. As a result, I ran out and bought every book he had written.

I put the book down and let the pent-up tears flow. I was so sad. The world I had envisioned seemed impossible now. When I was pregnant with this baby girl, I had pictured the two sisters dressed in matching pinafores with braided hair. They would be standing on the lawn, locked arm in arm, as their father photographed them. Hospital gowns and a bald head never entered my mind. More than sad, I was angry. In my mind in that moment, the sleeping child beside me was not going to have the chance for a full life. She was absolutely beautiful and possessed a gentle spirit. Had the suffering at such a young age changed her from a typical toddler who would get into everything, into one who was content to quietly play by herself? When my husband and I asked the doctors if they thought she was going to survive, they would only skirt the question. Skirting meant "no" to me. I put the book down and prayed; but it wasn't a pretty prayer like the prayer the man in the book had prayed. It was an angry prayer addressed to the highest point in my visual field.

"I've done everything I know," I told the ceiling. "I give up! It's up to you now."

In my heart, I knew the prayer was a two-pronged one: a prayer for the recovery of our sick child and a prayer for me. My many efforts at building a perfect world in which happiness would reign had not been successful.

At the very moment of the prayer, unbeknownst to me at the time, Someone else started running. "Run, run, God was running as fast as he could, for he saw one of his own children turn and start coming toward him" (my paraphrase of Luke 15:20).

I got through the rest of the day; my husband came home and the two of us put the children in their beds for the night. I could finally catch up on the work that had been neglected that day for taking care of a sick baby. It was then, alone in the family room folding clothes, that the Holy Spirit came to me in a tangible experience. I had run all of my life on self-induced energy; now there was a new kind of energy. Later, I would learn its name: *joy!*

All the running for happiness was also replaced by an emotion that is not dependent upon circumstance. *Peace* is its name.

Tangible peace and joy entered my soul. Because I can pinpoint these two God-given emotions to that very night, I have never second-guessed what happened: Our baby's hair grew back and there were pictures on the lawn! Then another sister and brother entered the frame. By the hand of God, the first prong of the prayer was answered and our daughter survived.

And what about the second prong of the prayer? The mother became a child that day, a child of God. I firmly believe we cannot be fully functioning adults unless we have had a childhood. God is now my heavenly Father in every sense. He also fulfills the role that is often assigned to a mother; he is my Counselor and Comforter. I can sit with him and ask him anything, tell him anything, cry with him, laugh with him. He is my Abba. Abba came running that day when I stopped. It took many years beyond my daughter's sick bed before I came to a full understanding of my newly-acquired status made possible by the Baby in the manger who fulfilled every promise of the Father. I can testify to the fact that I would not have been able to be the mother my children needed without the love that has flowed from the cross. A fabrication could never live on; Jesus is real because he lives on in every person who only finds his or her fulfillment in him. And he lives on in heaven to return again someday.

Grandmother had said, "Take up your cross." Luke's gospel records Jesus' words: "If any want to become my followers, let them deny themselves and take up their cross daily and follow me" (Luke 9:23, NRSV). This is the journey we are all called to take. The word in that scripture which made it come alive for me is "daily." I did not turn out to be a perfect person; just ask any of my four children. Daily I fail, and daily I need to remember to lean on God's grace. Because of the circumstances of my life, not a day passes that I don't need his grace. I could not reinvent myself or make a plan that would erase every unpleasant memory and ensure that nothing bad would ever happen.

The memories are still there and the crosses too; and there will always be more, because we live in a fallen world.

It is no longer my desire that my children say, "Our mother is perfect; she is such a dear." Now I desire that they will "arise and call me blessed" (see Proverbs 31:28). To be blessed is to be a receiver of God's grace. I desire to only witness God's love. By so doing, I will be leaving them the best possible legacy.

If I am ever honored to have one of my grandchildren come to me to share a corner of his or her heart, I will not be short on words—that is not my style. But in all my words, I hope I will be able to guide them to the only Way that will transform any noble dream into God's intended purpose.

A.R. Cecil is a wife of forty-one years. She and her husband, Joseph, have four grown children and four grand-children. She received a MSFA (Masters of Science in Fine Art) from the University of Wisconsin-Milwaukee. For several years, she wrote a column entitled "Journeys" for the Southeast Christian Church's newspaper. Mrs. Cecil has authored a collection of short stories, *That Was the Best Christmas!* (published by Cladach) and a collection of poetry and reflections, *In That Place Called Day*. She may be contacted at: inagreatfish@gmail.com. Learn more about A.R. (Alice) Cecil and her writings at www.GreatFishBooks.com.

2
SHE DID HER BEST
by Treva Brown

"God has said, 'Never will I leave you; never will I forsake you.'" -Hebrews 13:5

"*I'm really mad at Mom. I can't tell you one time when I felt close to her, like a mother-daughter feeling. I see my friends with their moms and I can see the relationship there and I'm jealous because I don't know how a mother-daughter relationship is. I was never close to Mom and it hurts me. I'm not saying I hate her, but I have not liked her for a long time. I didn't know her. She was a stranger to me and at times I felt uncomfortable around her. You know how mothers would bring little gifts to their daughters just out of the blue? You are the one that did it. Mom never gave me little cute things unless I asked her. She never thought about me the way you did.*"

This was an excerpt of a letter I wrote to my dad in 1992 when I was seventeen and hurting emotionally. This letter was written just five months after my mom died and my dad went to prison.

"Treva, your mom loved you more than life itself," Dad would say during our phone conversations. "She doted on you and always wanted the best for you. Please don't doubt your mother's love for you."

His pleading fell on deaf ears. I did not feel loved by my mother, so obviously she did not love me.

The summer of '92 was one I will never forget. June 1st

marked the last day of my junior year in high school. I walked out of those school doors just bursting at the seams to start my summer as an official senior. As I met up with my friends in the school parking lot, we started planning. One girl could not contain her excitement any longer and interrupted us.

"Can you believe it?" she said. "It is finally here ... the summer before our senior year!"

We all squealed at that exciting proclamation and took a moment to bask in all its glory. We were top dog now at our school and as seniors, we were in charge of planning the homecoming dance, senior prom, graduation, and not to forget our favorite, the senior class trip, which would take place the day after graduation. There was so much to do, but the most important at this moment was to enjoy our last summer together before going off to college. My friends and I were up for the task and eager to get started.

The first few weeks off I spent a lot of time hanging out with my friends and not much time with my parents. My dad was a truck driver so he was gone a few weeks at a time. My mom had a factory job and she chose to pick up extra hours causing her to work first and third shifts. She would be gone most nights. The nights she was working, I spent either with a friend or my grandparents. My grandparents' house was pretty much my second home. They had always supported their daughter and were never put out when Mom asked them if I could stay the night. My grandparents thoroughly enjoyed their grandchildren and were happy to oblige.

I remember a time when I asked my mom if I could have some friends over for a slumber party. She agreed and I started to make plans. At the last minute my mom told me to ask my grandparents if I could have the sleepover at their house because someone at her work could not make his/her shift, so she signed up to work it.

I was angry. This was not the first time I had asked to

do something and, though she agreed, she later backed out on me due to work.

"Sorry, but we need the money," was always her excuse.

How could I argue with that?

I called up my grandparents.

"Hello," answered my grandfather.

"Hi, Papaw. Can I ask you a favor?" I explained my situation with needing an alternative place for my slumber party because Mom had to work.

He had no problem with me bringing my party over to their house.

I was still a little disappointed that I had to change locations because my friends and I could not have the run of the house as we could have had at my house. However, I was grateful that my grandparents were always ready to accommodate. I'm not sure they looked forward to us teenage girls snickering and running to and from the refrigerator all hours of the night; but I do think they secretly enjoyed the full house again. Just as a typical sleepover goes, my friends and I stayed up late with the intent of sleeping in until at least noon.

That would not be the case for me this time. At 6:00 a.m. I was awakened by a tapping at my bedroom window. I got up and pulled back the curtain. I was shocked to see my dad. He was waving for me to come outside. Confused, I thought, *He's supposed to be on a road trip. Why in the world is he here waking me up so early?* I stepped outside to find out.

"What are you doing here?" I asked.

"Do you know where your mother is?" Dad was frantic.

"She signed up to work third shift for someone. She should be at work."

"She's not at work." He nervously shoved his hands in his pockets, then pulled them out again.

Dad's nervous behavior and fearful tone of voice struck some nerves of my own. A wave of fear came over me. My head started spinning with "what ifs." She had just started driving the heavy machinery at the factory. *What if Mom got into an accident at work? What if she got into a car accident on the way to work?* All those thoughts and more raced through my mind. Then I realized that Dad would have known if she were in an accident because he just came from her work. *So what is going on? Mom never skips out of work.* At this point, I needed to know where my mom was as much as my dad did.

"Will you drive around with me to look for her?" Dad interrupted my thoughts.

"Sure." I was eager to help him search. I stepped to go inside to get dressed and wake up my friends so they would know where I was.

"We don't have time. We have to go *now*." His urgent tone stopped me.

"Dad, I'm only wearing my nightgown and I'm barefoot!"

In a voice that sounded like a frightened child he said, "Please. Let's go now."

In my groggy, fearful state I agreed.

Shortly after we got on the road, we saw Mom driving towards us. She did not see us, so Dad swerved into her lane to force her to pull over on the side of the road. He rushed out the door to meet her; meanwhile, Mom got out of her car screaming at Dad at the top of her lungs.

I didn't know what to think. All I knew was that this episode was taking place a few blocks away from my high school and near houses in which some of my classmates lived, I was wearing my nightgown, and I had ditched my friends … again. My embarrassment took center stage over my fear.

My mom finally agreed to get into the vehicle Dad was driving. From the passenger seat, I turned around to speak to her as she slid into the backseat. As my eyes locked onto hers, I had a brief moment of terror. My own mother looked right at me without a look of recognition of who I was. She just stared at me as if in her mind she was asking herself, "Who is this girl looking at me?"

I was devastated. My mind was asking questions of its own: *What is wrong with my mom? How can she act as if she has no clue as to who I am?* I wanted to scream these questions at her, but I just sat there stunned with what my eyes were witnessing.

I looked more closely at Mom, then, and was sickened at what I saw. She was barely dressed and her hair was going every which way but right. Clearly, she had just rolled out of someone else's bed.

The three of us went back to our house and there I learned that my mom was having an affair with one of my dad's good friends. I knew this guy very well due to all the barbeques we had at his house. I also knew this man's reputation with the women. I was deeply ashamed that my own mother had become one of those women.

I do not remember the rest of that day; I only remember an overall feeling that stayed in our house after that moment of truth. Dad was crushed; Mom could barely look me in the eye out of her shame; and I, well I turned into one angry, disrespectful teenager.

I wish I could say that the only bad feeling I had towards my mom was that of shame, but it went deeper than that. I was angry towards her because her selfish actions were ruining what was supposed to be the best summer of my teenage years. In fact I thought she was purposely trying to sabotage my summer because the summer of her senior year in high school was cut short due to her being pregnant with me. Was this her payback to me because my birth stole her senior year in high school? That thought fanned the flame of my anger.

I felt hurt and confused. I needed my mom, but she was acting as if she did not want that role anymore. Her behavior crushed me more than I knew at the time. For the first time in my life, I felt as if I could not trust my own mother, who had obviously been lying to me for a long time. All these extra shifts that she claimed she was picking up were just a lie to cover for her affair. I lost respect for her.

In many ways I grew up admiring my mom. Though she got pregnant with me when she was sixteen, she never gave up on her dream of finishing high school. I still have the graduation picture of her decked out in cap and gown from head to toe—pride of the near impossible shown all over her face. I too have pride in her for never giving up. As a mother myself now, I know how exhausting it is when you see as much of the darkness of night as the light of day. Mom persevered. She always proved to be a hard worker. Whatever tasks the day held, she had each one checked off by nightfall. She also showed me how to not let feelings get in the way of accomplishments. No matter how tired she was from doing everyday household chores, tending to my needs and Dad's needs, she always got out of bed and arrived at work on time.

My mom had a wonderful gift. She had the innate ability to be self-taught in things that interested her. She could teach herself how to play a song on the piano without ever reading a note. She taught herself how to cook and sew, which landed her many jobs as a seamstress. She never had the best paying job, but she took pride in all she did. Unfortunately, none of these skills, such as sewing, cooking, or even playing the piano, were passed on to me. I thought maybe she didn't see any talent in me, that in her mind there was no way I could be capable of learning such things, so she didn't try to teach me. It was just one more reason for me to believe that my mom did not like me.

However, she was very good at providing all my necessities. And I always felt safe in her care. She was never a touchy-feely type or even one to say, "Hey, let's go grab an ice cream or something" just so we could have a heart-to-heart between mother and daughter. That was not her style. But I did admire her for her hard work, and while I did not always feel love from her, I felt a sense of the protection she offered.

My admiration, trust, pride, and respect for my mom all changed that early morning, as I sat in our vehicle, staring at a woman that I once called my mother. That was the day I realized I had lost my mom—even before she died.

As I mentioned earlier, I turned into an angry, disrespectful daughter—mainly towards my mom but also my dad. I was angry at him for treating my mom as a princess in the midst of her foolish antics. She was so consumed with herself, and Dad lavished her with so much attention, that I was just a passerby at times. My parents even overlooked my sweet-sixteen birthday. Once again, a time when I really hoped Mom would do something special for me, turned out to be another disappointment. I asked myself, *Why do I even hope anymore? My mom will never be like the other moms I see with their daughters.* All the emotion, disappointment, embarrass-ment, distrust, and shame I felt towards my mom all rolled up into one major ball of anger. When something set me off, that ball was thrown viciously towards my mom's heart. I unleashed my rage through words that dripped with venom.

One summer night I had made plans to go to a festival with my friends. I volunteered to drive, secretly wanting to show off the car my parents bought me. They had felt bad for not doing anything for my sixteenth birthday party, so they bought me a 1989 white Chevy Camaro. The car was a little beat up, but I didn't care. This car was my gateway to independence and freedom from all the drama my parents were creating in our house.

As I was skipping down the stairs towards the front door getting ready to leave, I got caught in the crossfire of my parents' latest war.

"Where do you think you are going?" asked my mom as if

she had never heard about my plans for the night.

I replied in a sarcastic tone of voice, "Mom, I told you days ago that I am picking up my friends and we are going to the Regatta."

My parents stared at me in disbelief as if they were never told of such plans.

I waited for the "aha" moment to show on their faces, but instead, my mom narrowed her eyes at me.

"Not tonight," she said.

"It's just not a good night, sweetheart," my dad said. He sounded sad; he knew how disappointed I would be.

"What do you mean, not tonight?!" I said a little hastily towards my mom, ignoring my dad altogether.

I felt the rage start burning in the pit of my stomach. Every time my parents warred with each other I felt thrown in the middle. Maybe they wanted to see whose side I was on. I never really understood their behavior. I did know that their constant arguing and emotional ups and downs were taking their toll on me. When I felt that familiar rage creeping up inside me, I would dash up to my room, slam my door, blast my stereo, and shout profanities at my mom.

This time, though, I shouted right into her face. "You always do this to me. I am so sick of it! I am so sick of you!" I cannot remember all I yelled at her that night but I do know my words were vicious and cruel.

I could see that I was hitting my mark by the hurtful look on her face. That only fueled me more. I wanted to hurt my mom the way she had been hurting me for the past few months.

"I hate you!" I shouted.

That was the final arrow aimed at her heart. I ran to my car, quickly got in, slammed the door, revved up the engine, and peeled out onto the street. I will never forget the pain I saw on my mom's face as I drove off. The last image I had of my mom alive was through my rearview mirror.

The anger that came over me that night did not allow me to feel remorse for my violent words. However, once curfew rolled around, my regret was growing. Sad to say, my regret was more because I knew I would face some type of consequence for my disrespect.

I dreaded the moment when I would hear those stern words from my parents, "Young lady, you are grounded for a month! No TV and no friends!"

I dreaded the consequence but I did not regret the harsh words I yelled. Those words were a true description of who my mom had become and I needed her to see that; I needed her to hear those words and my emotions behind them.

I dropped my friends off at their homes and finally arrived at my home by curfew. When I parked my car and walked up to the house, I saw no lights on. I crept into the house and up the stairs. Just as I was about to get into the safety of my room, I saw the TV on in my parents room. I poked my head in and only saw my dad. It was late, so I asked, "Where's Mom?"

"She's saying farewell to her affair so the three of us can be a family again."

I felt nauseous.

"Treva, would you sit with me and talk awhile?"

"Not tonight, Dad." With the events of that day, I was exhausted and, frankly, fed up with the drama. So, declining a chat with my dad, I went on to bed and fell asleep.

The next thing I knew, I heard dad in a crazed mess of tears, screaming out my mom's name. He came into my room saying that he had to go be with my mom and that I had to go to my grandparent's house. Once again, I had just awakened and was not sure what was happening. But the more gut-wrenching cries I heard from my dad, the more fear came over me. Dad was clearly hysterical; I could not understand what he was trying to say.

Finally his words were clear enough to understand.

"I love you, but I have to go be with your mom right now. Please get dressed and go to your grandparents."

He left my room, pacing the hallway between my bedroom door and that of my parents. Every so often, he would break into anguished tears.

"Baby, are you ready yet?" he would call through his tears.

I hurried as fast as my shaking hands allowed. I was ready outwardly to leave, but emotionally I wanted to stay with my dad. Still not knowing all the details, something inside my heart told me that this may be the last time I slept in this house with my parents.

I was finally dressed and my dad hugged me and wept, "Baby, I love you."

I was in such shock that I am not sure if I had a response. All I remember is feeling as if I did not want to leave my dad. I did as he asked and walked out our front door to leave for my grandparents' house a few miles away.

The moment I walked outside I saw that my house was surrounded by the police pointing their guns right at me. I froze in terror. I heard my aunt's voice and quickly ran to her. Still not knowing what fully happened between my mom and dad, I could tell that Dad was in big trouble. The next thing I knew, I was taken to the hospital where I was told my mom had been taken because of an injury she had suffered.

Not long after I arrived at the hospital, my aunt lovingly took me aside.

"Treva, do you know what has happened to your mom?"

"I'm not sure," was my dazed and confused answer.

I could tell what my aunt had to say next was something serious, causing her to choke back tears. She sat down beside me and grabbed my hand.

"Your mom has been shot in the head and it does not look good."

The moment I heard that, I knew what had happened due to the behavior of my dad a few moments ago.

My mom's side of the family and I stayed in that hospital for three days around the clock, leaving only to go back to my grandparents' house to clean up and grab a bite to eat. My two aunts on my mom's side, and another aunt that was my dad's younger sister, were constantly making sure I was OK. Periodically, they each would take me aside and ask, "How are you holding up? Is there anything I can get you?"

"No, thanks. I'm fine," I would say. They knew I was anything but fine; however, they gave me my space.

My best friend drove up to the hospital to visit me and said her mom had a message for me. She used the waiting room phone to dial her mom. Once her mom answered, she handed the phone to me. She insisted I come over to their house just so I could sleep in a comfortable bed. Again, I tried to hold onto my "tough" act and decline the gracious offer. She did not buy it one bit. She called me out saying, "Treva, you need some good sleep. I will have the bed ready and I expect you by dinnertime. We love you and we will see you soon." End of subject. I did not want to intrude, but secretly I needed to feel taken care of. My family was dealing with so much, that I felt as if I was not their number one concern; it felt nice to be parented.

By the fourth day the doctor's told us the brain damage was too extensive and Mom basically was gone. The only way her body had received oxygen was through machines. I overheard the doctors telling my grandparents where the bullet entered her brain and how there was no chance of survival. The moment the plug was pulled on Mom's life support, a realization hit me: My mom was dead because of a bullet that came out of a gun my dad fired!

I never got the chance to apologize to my mom for those harsh words. I never heard her explanation of why she acted as if she did not want to be my mom anymore. *Did she ever know how much I loved her, in spite of my disrespect towards her? Did she ever love me?* These thoughts plagued my mind day and night after she died.

I was able to have alone time with her as she lay lifeless in that hospital bed. The more I talked, trying to get some closure, the more uncomfortable I felt. *This is stupid,* I thought. *She can't even hear me.* I sat at the bedside just staring at her. I thought that if I held her hand or let her feel the tears pouring from my eyes, maybe she would show some sign of movement to let me know that she heard me. Nothing. Not one twitch, not one sound, nothing. That was the last time I spent alone with my mom. I could not bear one more minute knowing my mom was right there in front of me and yet not able to be a mother ever again. I would not go back into her room until a few days later when the doctor pulled the plug and pronounced her dead.

A whirlwind of events followed. The funeral had to be planned and then shortly after the burial, my dad's court case started. I remember few details of those months ... only the unlimited tears I poured out, the anger that consumed me, and the loneliness that threatened to suffocate me. I experienced, to the full, the stages of grief throughout these months. There were many days when I experienced all of these stages in just a few hours: denial, anger, bargaining, depression.

I was an emotional mess and getting worse. My family suggested that I should go see a counselor, but I refused. If I were to go talk to someone about the tragedy, then that would mean I was weak and I had allowed this to break me. I was adamant in showing everyone how strong I was and that this tragedy was not affecting me at all. I guess I wanted to prove to everyone that I was not messed up in the head. All I had ever wanted was a normal life, not the chaos that was so much a part of my childhood. I was driven to show everyone who

knew me that I was different and that I was going to have a
good life in spite of losing my parents in such a tragic way.

I had great friends who supported me day and night. They
really did their best to make me laugh, when I was on the verge
of tears, and just help me feel normal. My friends were the
support I desperately needed; my family was too consumed in
their own grief to help me. The grief my grandparents felt over
losing their daughter, and my aunts and uncles over losing their
sister, and the anger and unforgiveness they all had for my dad,
kept them unavailable to me. I was angry at them for many
years because I did not understand that they were grieving too.
There were many times when I needed my extended family to
just sit and talk to me, but they did not know what to say. All
they knew to do was give me my space. Those were the times
that made it unbearable not having my mom or dad near.

I did not like having those moments when I terribly missed
my mom and dad, so I would fill my mind with bad thoughts
about my mom. I would go back to the times when she lied
to me, when I felt she neglected me, or those times when I
could not recognize who she had become. My anger quickly
took over any grief I was feeling. That is how I mainly dealt
with losing my mom and dad. I chose to meditate on my angry
thoughts towards my mom, just so I would not break down
and cry. I was tired of crying.

Anger helped me to not completely lose my marbles.
However, I had a veil of anger over my eyes that kept me
from seeing the One who could help me. I felt immense anger
towards my mom, and also towards God.

"Why are you doing this to me?" I cried over and over to
a God whom I thought existed only to punish me. The guilt I
had felt over saying those awful words to my mom and having
those being the last words I spoke, or yelled to her, distorted
my view of who God really is.

I grew up in the Catholic church, going every Sunday or

Saturday with my Nan (grandmother). The majority of the time it was just her and me sitting in that third pew from the front. My attention was rarely on the Mass but occasionally the priest's words would catch my attention. Once I walked out those church doors, though, I forgot what I had heard.

My understanding of God was this: If I did everything right, then I would be taken care of, but if I did anything wrong, I was doomed. I had to always be on my best behavior or else God would not love me anymore. Because of my warped understanding of God, I lived for years after Mom's death blaming God for taking my parents away from me when I needed them most. I wanted nothing to do with him or religion. Well, let me rephrase that. The only thing I ever cared to do with God was to curse his name. My bitterness and anger caused me to give up on God. Thankfully, God never gave up on me. Hindsight really is 20/20. I can see so clearly today how God actively pursued me and protected me.

I was born and raised in West Virginia. Once I was catapulted out of my parent's "nest" when I was 16, it did not take me long to figure out that I needed a change of scenery. Even though I attended the university in my hometown, I realized that I was aimlessly wandering with no clear direction. I barely gained any college credits due to my irresponsible behavior; however, I did gain a solid friendship that has grown only stronger through the years, no matter the many miles between us. Thankfully my aunt, who lived in Florida, opened her home to me and suggested I go to massage therapy school until I figured out what career path I wanted to take. The one-way ticket out of my depressing town and the fact that massage school took only six months to complete, sold me in a heartbeat. In 1995, I moved to Florida. I completed a massage therapy program, took the state test to receive my licensing, and was hired as a massage therapist working in a medical setting. I was meeting wonderful people; most of whom were

Christians. I was always surprised at how much I enjoyed their company, seeing how I did not care for their beliefs. Many times I heard the stories taking place in their lives, and they always recognized God in the midst of them.

"Wow, that's cool," I would politely respond. I felt my role was to politely listen but not partake in full conversation when they spoke of God. I have to admit, since these patients were facedown on my table as I worked on their back, I did many eye rolls to their comments of how great God was. I would constantly think, *These people are crazy for believing in and being excited about a God who doesn't care if bad things happen to them.* Eventually, though, I found myself looking forward to seeing their names on my schedule for the day. The Christians I knew seemed to be confident about life, unlike myself and the crowd I normally hung around with. We were always questioning things of life and trying our hardest to figure it all out. Most of my days, I felt chaotic inside, never having peace. But when I worked on those patients who had a strong belief in God, peace surrounded me.

I never spent time with my patients outside of work, but I did become great friends with a co-worker. She held that same confidence and peace; she was completely in love with Jesus. I connected with her on an emotional level, though, because she too had a lot of unfortunate things happen to her. What appealed most to me about her was that even throughout all the turmoil she was experiencing in her personal life, she still spoke about God as if he was right there helping her, not harming her. During our chats, I would fire questions at her.

"You don't seem like a religious person and yet you speak of God as if he is your life, your everything."

"God is not about religion." Her tone was light, not harsh nor judgmental. "God is about relationship."

"How do you know there is a God? How can you believe he is helping you if you are still going through all this?"

"Because God says in the Bible that he is our help in times of trouble and I believe God's Word is true," she would say. She would end with a statement of fact: "God is for us, not against us!"

I never responded to that answer, but I refused to believe it.

My friend and I had many conversations about God. She never preached at me, only spoke about Jesus through her own experiences and would expand on the Bible only if I asked. As our friendship grew, I found myself asking more and more.

The more I would hear about God's love, the more restless I became. I had no idea at the time that the restlessness I felt was the Holy Spirit's way of preparing my heart to invite Jesus into my life. All I knew at that time was that something was not right inside me. My anger was not stopping my tears anymore as my mind constantly played memories of my mom, over and over. I came to the point where I was scared of actually losing my mind into the world of insanity.

It was Mother's Day and I was home alone. I was living with one of my best friends, who through her insightfulness will forever hold a special place in my heart. She was at her mother's house for this special day of honor. For the few years we were roommates, my friend was so thoughtful and caring, she would always invite me to join her on Mother's Day so I would not be alone. She knew how hard this day had become for me and did not want me to sit alone in my grief. I thought I would be that dreaded third wheel, so I always declined and reassured her that I was fine.

The moment my friend left to go spend the day honoring her mom, was the moment I broke down. I stayed in my bedroom and cried for almost a complete twenty-four-hour period. Looking back, I realize that, by my co-worker speaking the living Word of God to me almost on a daily basis, God's Word had started a crack in the thick wall of anger that held my heart captive. No matter how hard I tried, I could no longer focus on the anger my mom caused me. My mind now camped on the good times I had with her and my heart could not bear her absence. I knew I had to do something or else my days would be spent in a room with padded walls. I don't know what scared me more, the thought of being in a psych ward or the fact that once that happened, everyone would know I was a fraud. I could hear the talk of the town now.

"She was never strong, only weak," they would say. "We knew it would be a matter of time before she snapped just like her parents did."

The next day I was tempted to call and get out of work. I was exhausted. I looked as if a Mack truck ran me over and drug me clear to the next town. But something inside me propelled me forward. I knew I had to go to work. So I did. It was a slow morning. I was able to discuss my episode with my co-worker and she gently nudged me toward Jesus. I walked back to my office, sat down in my chair, bowed my head, and cried out to God. This time I did not curse his name or ask him "Why?" I simply poured out my heart.

"Jesus, please forgive me for all the bad I have done. I need you in my life. I don't understand you or the Bible, but I know I need you. Thank you, Jesus, for saving my life. Amen." As I lifted my head I realized I was smiling. I had not genuinely smiled in such a long time.

I also felt as if an immense weight was lifted off my shoulders and was replaced with pure joy. My life was still a mess, but I felt hope for the first time in many years. I did not understand, but somehow I did know that Jesus is real and he responded to my childlike prayer. It was a moment I will never forget.

God had to take baby steps with me when it came to my healing. I had so much anger, bitterness, unforgiveness, and guilt accompanied with self-loathing. The first layer of healing started right away with his proving to me that the Bible is his living Word. I had purchased a study Bible in a translation I could understand. Before I opened it to really try to read and understand what I was reading, I prayed.

"Jesus, I know you are real, but I do not know that the Bible is real. Please help me believe." I grabbed a section of the Bible, flipped it open, and my eyes locked on a verse that touched my wounded soul. It was Psalms 27:10:

> "Even if my father and mother abandon me, the LORD will hold me close" (NLT).

God did know that I felt abandoned. And he just told me that he really was holding me the whole time. My mind raced back to that year I lost my parents. I kept seeing flashes of times when I could not deny God had held me, comforted me, or kept me safe. I was brought to my knees in humble tears.

"God I am so sorry," I pleaded over and over. How could I have allowed my anger to keep me from the One who has always loved me through the pain? That was the day I realized my view of God was definitely warped. He was not a God of punishment as I had believed. God really has been *for* me and never *against* me. He is a God of pure love, who had been seeking a genuine friendship with me this whole time. I quickly learned a portion of God's nature, knowing that he is a gentleman who will never force me into a friendship with him. He had always given me the choice to say yes or no because he wants my heart, not just my actions.

I still had more truth to learn in order to erase all those lies I had believed about myself and my mom, but now I was willing. I took action by reading the Bible on a daily basis. I also learned to not just read it, but to apply it to my life's situations, in order for me to see change. Jesus gave me the tools and power to change, but I had to receive it and apply it.

The first change I needed was to stop throwing a self-pity party every time something seemed hard to me. For example, I've always had a weakness in the area of budgeting my finances. In my miserable state I would want to give up and say, "Well, if I had a mom who cared enough to teach me that skill, I could do this. But she didn't teach me, so there is no way I can. I'm just not good at it." I get a sick feeling in my stomach even now as I write this. My attitude was so pitiful!

God revealed to me that I had to stop blaming my mom for everything that was hard or went wrong in my life—which also meant I had to forgive her. I did not know how to start that process, but God brought wonderful people into my life during this time of healing.

Within a year of my decision to receive Jesus as my personal Savior, I started working at another doctor's office and met a co-worker there who became one of my closest friends. She and I both struggled with our relationships with our moms and we became each other's support in this journey of forgiving our mothers. God gave us wonderful parent figures—parents of another, mutual friend of ours. This couple embraced us as their second and third daughters. Through them I gained much more understanding of who God is and grew in my faith. I will forever be grateful that God orchestrated that time in my life. He gave me a friend who has been the closest thing to having a sister, and he placed me in the gentle care of my "Florida parents," as I call them, to help me start the process of healing.

Forgiving my mom was not easy and there was some real pain associated with the process. Even though I had a great support group with my circle of friends, I still had to seek therapy with a professional Christian psychologist. She helped me to sort through all the negative emotions and help me feel OK with the positive emotions I had towards my mom. I eventually came to a place in my heart where I could think of the good memories I had of Mom without completely breaking down in a mess of tears.

My counselor and I tackled the subject of anger towards my dad too. Forgiving him had never been much of an issue. I knew my dad better than anyone else, and in my heart I always knew this act was not something he premeditated. It was an act driven by extreme hurt and other strong emotions. My dad is not a murderer at heart, and I always knew that.

The main issue I had to deal with regarding my dad was the fact that I had to go into a prison to have a relationship with him. I hated everything about that process. Just the fact that I had to fill out a form with personal information on it, have complete strangers review it, and know that it was their decision whether or not I was approved to see my father, caused me to feel completely violated. That did not sit well with me. I had to work through anger towards my dad for putting himself in a situation that led him to a place where barriers stood in the way of our relationship. The fact that Dad and I had always had a great father/daughter relationship made it easier for me to want to visit him in prison, though. Once I got past the coldness of the processing area in that drab, gray building, and walked through the heavy steel door, I would see my dad at our assigned table waiting for me. In an instant, all was well with the world. Seeing him always warmed my heart. We would quickly resume our relationship, never missing a beat.

Trying to have a normal relationship with my dad inside a prison, where there are numerous rules, guards constantly watching, and trying to focus on our visit while having so many other people around, was extremely hard at times. But the hardest part of it all was leaving my dad behind. He and I would notice visiting time was coming to an end and start to inch our way up to the door. Dad would give me a big hug. I could feel him tremble and hear the tremor in his voice.

"I love you, baby. I am so proud of you," he would say.
I would do my hardest to choke back my tears.

Though my dad's actions had hurt me greatly, forgiving
him came easy because of my love for him. I prayed for him
unceasingly. In my Bible studies or small groups, I made it
a point to include my dad when I was asked for my prayer
requests. I was not going to give up until I knew my dad
was free from the chains that bound his mind and heart.
Even though I knew his physical freedom was taken away, his
freedom in Christ was my priority.

Thankfully after many years of talking to Dad about Jesus,
praying and fasting for him, I received a letter from him
around Christmas time. In it he wrote:

> "I surrendered my life to Christ and baby, I feel so free. Why
> did I ever hate the One who always loved me?...I know I have a
> long road of healing, and people may never forgive me for what
> I did, but I am so sorry I caused so many so much pain....Thank
> you, Treva, for never giving up on me."

I keep that letter in my Bible as a constant reminder that
my dad is now free through the power and forgiveness of Jesus.

It was such a reality of God's power when I first witnessed how God has changed my dad. There was a situation
that happened to my dad in prison where he would normally
have said and done the wrong thing. But as he told me this
situation, he spoke with wisdom and love. He was definitely
being wronged, but he fully trusted God and let *him* handle
the details. I was in awe as I sat there listening to my dad
as a changed man.

My dad played a big part in helping me to forgive my
mom. I knew it broke his heart every time I spoke ill about her,
but he sat quietly, letting me vent. When he knew I had gotten
out all my frustration for the moment, he would gently tell me

about a loving act my mother showed towards me. Depending on my mood, I would either change the subject or ask more about that particular time my mom loved on me. I had to admit, it was nice hearing him recall such sweet memories.

The day came when I knew God wanted me to write my mom a letter, seeing how writing allows me to pour out my soul. Here is a piece of that letter I wrote to Mom on the anniversary of her death that helped me to release the last bit of anger I was holding towards her:

"After you died I was a wreck. The years following your death are years I am not proud of. I hated life, I hated you. I wanted to forget you, yet I was scared to do so."

The letter starts describing how I asked Jesus to be a part of my life and how his healing brought me to this point of forgiveness:

"Why did our family not know Jesus? As parents it was yours and Dad's responsibility to lead a life directing me to the grace of God. I understand now why you didn't, and by that you have given me unspoken advice. I suppose a lot of what you and Dad gave me was unspoken advice. I don't want to be that way towards my children, if I ever have any."

I jump around some in the letter, but I come to a point where I unlocked the chains of my heart and released my anger towards my mother.

"Mom, it's been hard. I've needed you here with me from the first moment you left me. You gave up being a mom to me way before you died. And I don't understand that. I've hated you a long time for that. I don't hate you now. Mom, do you think I would be a good mom? It makes me nervous sometimes when I think about it. I do hope I'll get the chance."

There is much more to this letter. It touches my heart even now, several years later. This letter holds physical proof of releasing my mom and receiving healing: The pages are stained with the many teardrops that fell as I wrote. I remember the pain of writing it; because of all the great things God had brought into my life at that point, I wanted her to see and be a part of them. Instead of a face-to-face conversation with her, I had to write a letter, one that would never be received.

Once I finished writing the letter, though, I felt free. It felt as if something was taken off me and I fully released the anger I held towards my mom. I finally had closure. Something else happened too. Once anger stopped blocking my view, it was as if God gave me insight into what my mom was going through the last few years of her life. I started seeing her in ways I had never seen before. It doesn't make it right how she treated me, or the choices she had made, but I started to empathize with her and could understand some of her reasoning behind her actions. I finally and fully knew it was not my fault. She just made bad choices that unfortunately I had to live with as well, but it was not my fault. Again, freedom poured into my soul.

At the time I wrote the letter, I had just married my husband and we did not have our children yet. Today, I am married to an amazing man who, thankfully, God brought my way. We recently celebrated our ten-year wedding anniversary, and we have three children who have overtaken our hearts. I think of the love and commitment my husband and I share with one another, and sometimes it makes me sad that my parents missed out on that with each other. I am so thankful that God healed me to the point of having the type of relationship with my husband and my children that he designed.

Even though God healed me, there was a moment when my insecurities of being a mom crept in. I remember when I was pregnant with my firstborn. I was in the third trimester. I didn't know which was bigger, my belly or my feet! I had just sat down to try to ease the achiness of my lower back, and my mind started going down a path that caused anxiety to well up within me: *What if my child grows up feeling like I do not love him, the way I felt about my mom? Is he going to hate me? Am I going to cause him emotional pain?*

My negative thoughts seemed endless. I walked into the kitchen for a glass of water and my eyes instantly locked onto a plaque my husband had hung beside the kitchen sink. The plaque reads: "Trust in the LORD with all your heart; do not depend on your own understanding" (Proverbs 3:5, NLT).

Because I did not have the healthiest role model in mothering, my fears invaded my mind for a moment until my eyes locked on the truth—God's truth. I did not know how to be a parent, but I chose to trust the ultimate parent, our heavenly Father, and follow his lead. Today, when I struggle in my parenting, my prayer is, "God, I need your guidance here. I do not know what to do, but I believe you know." I follow that prayer up with another: "God, please protect my children from my inadequacies." And I rest in the peace that comes, wholeheartedly knowing that God is faithful.

My mom struggled with being a parent too. After all, she was just a child herself when she gave birth to me. Unfortunately she chose to not ask God for guidance. Even though it did not come easy for her to show me love in ways that I could recognize and receive, she did provide for me. Through this process of healing, I realize now that her provision was her way of expressing her love for me.

Even as I write, God is taking me to another level of healing. As I recall more and more good memories of the times my mom and I shared when I was a little girl, I no longer feel that deep sadness. I have actually smiled about many of those memories! That would have never happened years ago. Thank you, Jesus, for helping me receive your power for my life.

One of those sweet memories I am able to recall happened when I was in elementary school. I had very long hair as a child. People always made a point to compliment my mother, saying things like, "Oh my! Your daughter's hair is so long and beautiful." I saw my mom's eyes glisten with pride with every compliment. Many nights, she would take time to sit and brush my hair. With every stroke of the brush, out came the tangles of my active day. As much as I despised this brush session, only because I had a very tender head, I looked forward to the moments spent with my mom. Sometimes she would be so tired that we would mostly sit in silence. That was still OK, because just the closeness of her eased all the tension I may have felt that day. But other times, Mom and I held a comfortable chatter, talking about our day. She would ask, "So how was your cheerleading practice today? Did you learn any more cheers?" And I would reply with a detailed description of my day, including much more than just my cheerleading practice. She knew her simple question was a way to open the doors of my otherwise introverted personality. I would then ask her about her job. Even though she never had a great-paying job, she enjoyed her work. I always liked hearing her stories. It was a great way to wind down before bedtime.

After my hair was tangle free, Mom would say, "We are all done. Now what book are we going to read tonight?" After the story, she would tuck me in bed and before she left my bedroom, she would gently sweep her hand under my head, lifting all that hair of mine off to the side so I would not be lying in a heap of hair. It was one of my favorite things she did for me. To this day, I do the same thing to my four-year-old girl who has followed in my footsteps with that long, beautiful hair. As I grew up, I eventually cut my hair, but no matter how long or short it was, that was our special ritual most every night my mom and I were together.

Through God's healing—and help from my dad—I am now able to recall more memories of the loving things my mom did for me as a child. I am proud of her for taking what little she had and offering it to me. I can honestly say that for the few years I had her, my mom did her best.

Treva Brown no longer lives a grief-stricken life, but a victory-driven life, due to her personal relationship with Jesus Christ who is the Ultimate Healer of our grief. Treva has a heart for those who are hurting, especially those affected by uxoricide (murder of a wife by her husband). She is writing a book to show grieving children of uxoricide that life did not end for them too, and they do not have to walk that painful road alone.

Treva is also passionate about Mothers of Preschooler's, a ministry that encourages moms in their parenting and faith, letting each mother know that they are not alone. She serves as social coordinator on the steering team of her local MOPS group. Treva is a wife and mother of three living in Colorado. She maintains a blog at http://treva-brown.blogspot.com/.

3
TAKE CARE OF YOUR MOTHER
by Verna Hill Simms

"When Jesus saw his mother there, and the disciple whom he loved standing nearby, he said to her, 'Woman, here is your son,' and to the disciple, 'Here is your mother.'" -John 19:26-27

"Mail for Simms!" The call came from downstairs; a mysterious, unopened letter. How irresistible.

"Shall we go see what it is?" I asked my seven-month old daughter, Dee Dee. In answer she raised two small arms, and her face brightened with a big smile as she blew happy bubbles. I lifted her in my arms and held her close. I relished the fresh aroma of her freshly washed honey-colored hair.

At the foot of the stairs my landlady handed me an envelope with Mother's handwriting. My shaky knees barely allowed me to sit on the bottom step. Dee squirmed, crawling from my arms onto the thick rose-colored carpet she loved.

"Oh!" I stammered. "It's from Mom. My brother must be gone. The draft has taken him. Why else would she write?"

The older woman's wrinkled face held a concerned expression. "Is that the nice young man that brings your mother to visit every Wednesday? Not many sons are that attentive," she added.

I nodded. "Yes, that's Lewis." A slight quiver sneaked into my voice. Lewis was twenty-four and my older brother. Both

58

my husband and brother worked at Small Arms, an ammunition plant in St. Louis, not far from our apartment. Lewis drove a carpool forty miles to work five days a week and had foregone an extra paying passenger to make room for our mother to ride. In 1942, a horrible war raged across the ocean and every single, eligible young man was soon drafted.

I knew Mom didn't have a telephone and wouldn't knock on a neighbor's door and ask to use theirs. Tears rolled down my cheeks. Hastily ripping the envelope, I inflicted a paper cut on my hand. No matter. I sucked the wound as I read the letter. It said, "Lewis left for boot camp today." It was hard for me to visualize this gentle brother wearing a uniform and carrying a gun. I wiped tears from blurry eyes with the back of my hand before continuing to read:

"My prayers could not spare him this terrible ordeal. You know that your brother has been my sole support and companion for six years, taking me wherever I needed to go. Now the house is empty. He shouldn't have extra worry about my safety and welfare, while he is miles away fighting the enemy. Ask your husband if I can live with you and him until the war is over? Love, Mom."

The letter slipped from my shaky hands and dropped to the floor. *Oh, Dad, what have you done to your children?* Eleven years fell away. In memory I became ten years old once more...

We had been traveling for over a week in an old truck and had finally arrived—two weary adults and their three fidgety children.

The evening shadows were long as the sun dipped below the treetops.

"Almost there," Dad assured us. "I've kept my promise. We're now driving on our land in Missouri." It was June 5, 1931, Mama's fiftieth birthday.

Years ago, my parents made an agreement. If Mama would

allow him to sell the farm in Missouri and move to Arizona, then after ten years, if she was dissatisfied, they would return. The band of five, my parents and three children—Irene the oldest at fifteen—had traveled eight days, sleeping nights in a flat homemade trailer covered with canvas. We had left my two oldest brothers, now grown, in Arizona.

Each night during our travels, the family knelt on the running board of the truck: "Oh Lord, thank you for the many blessings in life. Be with us and keep us well and safe on the journey ahead. May we count on your protection as we close our eyes in sleep? We ask these blessings in Jesus' name. Amen."

I squirmed in my seat, so excited to actually be here! All eyes opened wide as the truck bumped along in low gear—down-down-down, crossing a shallow, rocky, creek bed—before laboring up a slight incline and braking to a stop.

I exhaled and stuck my head out the open window. The slight breeze on my short brown hair felt good and tickled my ears. I could smell the fragrance of cedar trees.

"A creek!" I squealed. "Is it ours? It looks clean. Can Lewis and I wade?"

"Not tonight, Verna." Mama's voice sounded hollow, as if it had come from far away. She removed a hairpin from her dark-brown topknot and jammed it back in—a nervous habit I had noticed when she was upset.

Five people exhaled. Our new home! In the middle of the Great Depression little money was available. Dad had traded (sight unseen) our house in Tempe, Arizona, for this acreage. It included a two-room cabin nestled in the Ozarks, seven or eight miles north of Norwood, Missouri. The real estate company had listed it as a farm with fruit trees, a spring, and fertile tillable land.

A mass of beautiful orange poppies, in full bloom, covered the yard. Their beauty amazed me. "Oh, flowers, my favorite

color: orange. Aren't they pretty?" I glanced at Mama to share
my pleasure. She turned her head away, trying hard to keep me
from seeing the tears leaking from her tired eyes.

What Mama was seeing was a one-room, windowless,
log cabin with a small lean-to. The only openings were two
closed doors. Numerous cracks left by chipped and fallen
mortar let flickering lights escape from an oil lamp burning
inside.

Dad stared straight ahead, jaws working. His clenched
fists and knuckles turned white against dark suntanned skin.
Such a house!—and to make matters worse—occupied by
squatters. Grabbing a hunting rifle, he turned to us and
ordered, "Remain seated." The truck's door slammed force-
fully and we four stunned occupants sat rigid in stony
silence. No gunshot or loud noises were heard. With no
explanation from our parents, we slept one more night in
the trailer that was still hooked to the truck.

Sounds of sawing awakened me the next morning. The
sun beamed down in my eyes. I squinted as I emerged from
my bed, fully clothed, and looked around. I saw Dad had
removed the truck's windshield. Sweat ran down his face as
he used a handsaw to cut through logs on the south wall
of the cabin. My brother, Lewis, sat hunched over, stoking
a fire built under our old iron kettle. Irene stood bracing
her legs while holding a water bucket under the flow of an
artesian well.

"What's Daddy doing?" I asked, walking over to where
she stood holding the filled bucket with both hands. I
reached over to the well and splashed cool water on my
face.

"Mother is unhappy about not having any light in the
cabin. Dad lost his temper and is going to install the truck's
windshield for a window. Better not ask them questions.
Everyone is angry and in a bad mood." She hesitated before

adding, "The couple left at daybreak—taking their few possessions with them."

And so, down in the "holler" on the farm in Missouri, our new life began.

The summer dragged on, with us three children picking up rocks and carrying them to Dad. He planned to build a low wall around the farm. I remember him muttering, "Couldn't plow this dirt even if we had a horse and plow. Rocks strewn everywhere. And they call this fertile soil!"

One fall morning that first year, Dad announced, "I'm moving to Springfield. My aunt lives in a house needing repairs. Here's a twenty, Cora. I don't know when, or if, I'll return."

He studied our bewildered faces. He said, "Lewis, you're twelve, getting close to thirteen. You'll be a man then, and I'll expect you to take care of your mother. Bye." He jammed a black felt hat over the slight wave in his hair.

I looked up at the sky, not wanting to see Dad's sour expression. The cleft in his chin seemed to have deepened with his mood. I hoped for rain, a storm—anything to protest this new development in my life.

We four stood outside the doorway and watched horrified until the truck splashed through our little creek at the base of the hill, and drove up the other side out of sight and sound. Irene's usual smiling face frowned as she ran her fingers through her shoulder length hair and turned away. Mama's resigned expression told us we would not see our other parent for a long time.

Mama was the first to speak. "Wish he'd have built an outhouse before he left."

"I'll construct it," Lewis said, brightening, "if I can borrow tools from a neighbor." He walked to the other side of the house and we followed. "Where do you want it? I'm thinking a little ways up the hill." No one answered. "It might be handier on the lower side but down there's the only good garden spot. Nothing can grow near those large oak trees. What do you think?"

"You choose a spot, Lewis. But first come in the house." Mama reached for his hand and pulled him with her. "I knew he wouldn't stay, so I hid these." She leaned over and pulled a cardboard box from under her bed. Her face beamed as Lewis removed the lid to see a saw, hammer, screwdriver, and a large crowbar. A hatchet, shovel, and hoe made up the rest of our survival tools.

"Do you think you could make a rabbit trap first? We need meat. I'll draw a picture of one we had on the farm." Mama didn't wait for an answer but opened the dresser drawer for paper and pencil.

From that day forward she assumed her children could do anything. My brother became head of the household and tried hard to do all that was needed.

"Where will we get money to buy lumber?" Irene asked, tossing her straw colored hair.

"I saw an old fallen-down barn on the far side of our land," Lewis said. "It should provide plenty of wood for projects."

Later, Lewis grunted as he pried boards loose. "I didn't know this old oak lumber would be so hard." Tying them to a child's wagon, we took turns pulling and pushing until we reached the hole Lewis had dug for our toilet. I held the wood in place for Lewis to saw and nail. We didn't have money to buy nails either.

"Save the nails I pull, Verna, and straighten them on a flat rock," he ordered, without stopping his sawing and hammering.

That year we learned to improvise. We were proud of our crude handiwork, even if there was no door to the little building. It faced away from the house, didn't it?

With Papa and the truck gone, we walked everywhere.

The next Sunday at church, someone asked, "Where is your man?"

Mama didn't go into detail. "He's working in Springfield," she said. But the country folks were wise in the ways of men and guessed he had deserted the family. One by one they offered to help. Neighbors on the north hill sold cream for butter and owned a separator. They gave us part of the skim milk that was left, before pouring the remainder in a trough for the pigs. Irene carried a gallon home each day. In my mind's eye I can still see her blue eyes sparkling and hear her singing as loud as she could while walking up the hill swinging a bucket. I'm sure her song could be heard all over the farm. People living to the east shared their abundance of a tomato crop, and the good folks on the west said, "We never use all of the dropped apples. Come and help yourself to all you want."

"I'll pull my farm wagon up to their orchard and bring the fruit home," Lewis volunteered. "Verna can help." It was never, "Will you, Verna?" And Mama seemed to agree. I knew it was necessary; but over the years I began to feel Mama favored Lewis over me and I couldn't help but resent it. I was working hard too, wasn't I? Shouldn't I get some credit?

But no matter—we had to eat—and so I helped to gather all that was offered, picked wild grapes for jelly, harvested walnuts from the ground, wild blackberries for canning or making cobbler, and some raspberries. Mama sliced and peeled apples and placed the raw fruit on sheets in the hot attic to dry. We shucked corn planted by the squatters and hauled dried kernels to the mill to be ground into cornmeal, on shares. Dried beans, stuffed into a sack, were beaten before throwing the crushed pods into the air. Wind blew away chaff, leaving the heavier beans for storage and winter's use.

"What are you doing, Lewis?" I exclaimed, coming up behind him one afternoon to see nails being driven into the kitchen threshold.

Lewis laughed, "Oh, our wind-up clock isn't dependable anymore. I'm making sort of a sundial. It's not very good but at least we can tell when it is eight, noon, and four o'clock."

I was not impressed. Sometimes my brother's ideas were too much! "What if the sun doesn't shine?"

He replied, "Of course when we have no sunshine, we'll have to guess what time to go to school, walk up the hill for milk or our mail."

Lewis looked grumpy so I walked away, but not in time to miss his grumble: "I'm doing the best I can."

Mama seemed pleased with Lewis's idea, and bragged on how clever her son had become.

For fourteen months we lived off the land and grew strong and healthy before drought forced us to move into town— where Mother and Irene found work.

Years passed. We had very little contact with Dad after he left, but we did learn that he had married a younger woman and was busy fathering another group of children and had no time or interest in us.

One fall evening we four sat around the kitchen table. A sparkling, white cloth set off the chocolate cake decorated with green candles. Lewis's sixteenth birthday.

"Let us pray," Mama said, bowing her head. "Our Father in heaven, we beg your blessing on the food set before us. May it give us health and nourishment. I pray for your continued guidance in raising my children and ask that you free them from the temptations of the world, and keep my son safe as he drives the busy highways. We ask all in Jesus' name. Amen."

Lewis's head shot up, "How did you know I planned to quit school, work full time, and buy a car? With wheels I will drive you to work every day."

"No!" Mama shook her head. "I will not allow it. Irene and I have saved a hundred dollars between us. Her boss told her that is enough for a vehicle. You must and you will finish school."

So a black Model A Ford was purchased and Lewis and Irene learned to drive. Then, the day Lewis graduated from high school, he said, "Mom, you have worked long enough. Quit your job. I will take care of you now." And he did, until … World War II.

And then, on that day when the letter arrived announcing that Lewis had been drafted, the torch of responsibility was handed to me. I admit I didn't want it. I liked being free—with just my husband, Howard, and a child to care for. I cherished the privacy of living in a three-room apartment, with only the three of us, my husband and little baby girl.

Yet, my good husband agreed that we should take care of my mother; and that day a new life began for all of us. We gave up our bedroom to my mom and moved our bed into the living room. Would Mother and I get along—two grown women in one small apartment, both of us used to having our own way?

And then an unexpected thing happened. One weekend we sat visiting my husband's parents in Festus, a town about forty miles south of St. Louis. I'm not sure how it was decided, but it suddenly dawned on me that we had agreed to let Howard's sister also move in with us. She wanted to work in St. Louis while her husband was off at war and needed a safe place to live.

"Where will Norma sleep?" I asked.

"Your mom has a double bed. Should be plenty of room."

My heart dropped down into the pit of my stomach. We'll have a civil war right here in my home. Three independent women under one roof! And two of them not related.

Surprisingly it worked out. Everyone cooperated and as time passed I began to see the benefits of such an arrangement.

Norma paid a small boarding fee and helped with the dishes. She also spent time with the baby. Mother became a free babysitter for the days when I needed to shop, or for the evenings Howard, Norma, and I ran to catch a streetcar, so we could see the early movie when rates were cheaper. There was always a newsreel showing moving pictures of the horrors overseas.

All of us lived for the news on the radio and the mail that came every day. I had two brothers in the service and two brothers-in-law. Norma had a husband and a brother. We had this one important worry in common and somehow it was a comfort to have the four extra hands to hold while we prayed together over the evening meal, and at nighttime when we appealed to our Creator to protect all those we loved.

And so the days turned into weeks, the weeks into months, and the months into years and the war raged on. The United States won some battles; the Germans and Japanese won an equal amount. We saw the victory sign with fingers formed in a V wherever we went. Gas, shoes, coffee, sugar, and meat were rationed. In order to buy toothpaste, we were required to return an empty tube. Tires for cars were unavailable, and we were asked to turn in any extra ones we had. Automobiles, stoves, refrigerators, or anything made from metal were not available for purchase. All metal was used to make weapons of destruction.

And then one day it happened—disaster—in the form of a letter to my husband: "Uncle Sam needs you!" Wasn't it bad enough? The government already had two of my brothers. Now they laid claim on my husband—father of my child—my only support. Would I have to leave my baby and go to work?

My whole world was suddenly turned upside down. Howard looked at me with a solemn face. "I'm not actually in the army yet, hon. Perhaps if I enlist in the Navy—they have a construction battalion, you know—and if I qualify maybe I won't have to kill anyone, but can serve erecting bridges. I'm an experienced pipe fitter. What do you think?"

So it was decided. He took off from work the next morning and enlisted. After passing a written test and a physical, he became a Seabee as the unit was called. Time flew by swiftly while we made preparations and enjoyed our last few days together, and then—one day he was gone! An empty hole remained in our lives for almost two years.

Norma moved back in with her parents; Mom and I had our furniture loaded on a truck and hauled to Festus, the town where we had lived before the terrible tragedy overseas involved the United States. I found employment and that helped with the bills. Mom took care of Dee. Each day dragged into the next with the same empty sameness.

We still didn't have a telephone, so there was a span of nine months when I didn't see or talk to my husband. We each wrote letters every day but there is only so much comfort in the printed word. Dee Dee's only memory of her dad became the man in the picture that she had been told was her daddy.

September 2, 1945: On that chilly morning I hopped out of bed and walked to work as usual. Our car had long ago given up the ghost and I'd been forced to carry the battery into the house and place it behind the heating stove to keep it from freezing.

At work, everyone was buzzing. "The war is almost over. Japan is in negotiations as we stand talking. Someone go in the office and check if any news is on the radio."

I don't think we did a lick of useful work that morning. When the boss came in at noon and held up both hand making two "V for victory" signs, we all cheered. He laughed his usual good-natured laugh. "It's over, everyone! Japan signed a formal unconditional surrender aboard the USS Missouri this morning. Take the rest of the day off and celebrate!"

Lewis and Verna as young children

My co-worker and I joined hands and danced around in a circle. I could scarcely contain my joy. I rushed home to spread the news to my family. I expected my husband home as fast as the trains could roll, but I was dead wrong. President Truman had announced it wouldn't do to bring all the men and women home at one time. Not enough housing and jobs. First drafted, first out. So again I played the waiting game.

Howard wasn't discharged until April 1946. The day finally arrived. Home at last! We were jubilant to see each other; but it wasn't all carefree happiness. The world he had left had changed. It became evident that those who had dodged the draft had fared much better. It was impossible to see healthy men with their fine cars and nice houses and not be a bit jealous.

And then, there was the ever-present problem of my mother. I felt I should be free of the responsibility now. Lewis promptly married a girl he had fallen in love with during boot training and moved to Michigan to be near her mother. My sister, Irene, and her husband worked in St. Louis and rented an apartment there.

I said to Irene, "Could you take Mom to live with you? I'd like to have another baby and don't need the stress of trying to keep everyone happy."

She agreed and rented Mom a small apartment in her building and everything went great for a year or two.

One day when I drove to St. Louis to visit Mom, she said. "Verna, I'm not happy living in the city. The air isn't pure. Irene is gone all day and I don't drive a car; the buses are crowded. And you don't know how much I miss your daughter. Find me a place in Festus."

I couldn't. Nothing was available, not one. There had been no building during the four years of fighting. Carpenters were putting up cracker boxes of dwellings but returning soldiers and their families occupied them all. And the houses were expensive. Prices had doubled since the beginning of the war.

Once more, my husband came to Mom's rescue. He found a lot for sale within easy walking distance of our home. He talked to Irene's husband and they agreed to pool their resources and furnish the labor to construct a two-room dwelling for Mom. Irene and I helped. None of us knew carpentry. If only Lewis would come and work with us. He knew his way around a saw and hammer. Finally the house was finished and Mom moved in.

The next time Irene saw our brother, she asked, "Why didn't you drive down to Missouri and help? Neither Joe nor Howard was a carpenter, and both worked full time at their regular jobs. They had a terrible time and wasted almost as much time driving around town looking at houses being built and asking the builders how to turn corner, etc. You don't know how much we could have used you, while trying to do the almost impossible."

Lewis looked surprised. "Didn't you know? Mother wrote and told me not to come until the house was finished. I don't know why. I thought it was your idea."

I was livid with rage. How could she? I'd always known Mom favored my brother, but this? It was way too much, way, way too much!

I started thinking more about the times when I thought Mother showed favoritism toward Lewis. I have an old photo of Lewis and me as little children. I love this picture as I loved my brother, but I've often wondered why he was dressed so much nicer than I was in the picture.

On the first day of school for both my brother and me—I was starting kindergarten and he was starting first grade—Mother went with him and my sixteen-year-old brother went with me. I don't recall it upset me; but as I looked back on it, it was a bit strange. Another time a friend invited my ten-year-old sister to spend the weekend at their summer resort cabin and Mother wouldn't let her go unless Lewis and I went along. They took us, but she was never invited again. When Irene was in sixth grade and Lewis was in second, the school had a Christmas party for Irene's class but not for Lewis's, so Mother made Irene take Lewis with her—but he cried and the teacher told Irene to take him home, so they both missed the party.

If Mother favored Lewis, why did she choose to live closer to me? Because I had two daughters to which Mother had developed a close bond. Lewis and Irene had no children at the time. Mother had been raised in Missouri and didn't like the climate in Michigan where Lewis lived. I was the only adult member of the family who didn't work away from home and was available to cater to Mother and haul her anywhere she needed or wanted to go. And lastly, Lewis and his bride didn't want the responsibility and work of another widow woman—they already had his wife's mother.

It was years before I completely forgave my mother. During the 1920s and '30s it was common for mothers to favor boys—they were her pride and joy. Girls were more of a necessity to help with the housework and serve the menfolk of the family. I didn't see the situation as anything unusual and didn't resent it until I was grown and had daughters of my own.

Then one night when I lay awake thinking of the past and all the sacrifices Mom had made for me, I decided to record everything for future generations. It dawned on me. Mom had enough love to favor Lewis and still plenty left over for me. And didn't I love Lewis also? I was being childish. I prayed for the guidance and grace to forgive—and it worked. I discovered that after I forgave her, I enjoyed the time we spent together. I have always been thankful I kept my hostilities to myself and never mentioned my hurt to Mom. After all, I had been taught to respect my elders and the Bible says to honor your mother and father so your days may be long upon the earth.

Both my brother and mother are dead now. When I think of one, I remember the other: a loving mother and a boy who took his dad's order very seriously: "Take care of your mother, Son."

After Mom died, I wondered where her wedding band and antique dishes were. I found out she had given them to Lewis. Though that would have bothered me in the past, now I could accept it.

I began the practice of writing a letter to her each year on her birthday. On June 1, 2006, I wrote:

Dear Mom,

As I sit at my computer composing this yearly birthday letter my mind travels back to the years when you lived on earth. Maybe you are here now, hovering above watching my fingers as they fly over the keys, hitting the wrong ones occasionally. I feel your presence more with my eyes closed, so I'll shut them now and together you and I will recall the past. ...

The years was 1947—a warm day in early spring. Dee had entered the first grade and as I returned from driving her to school I stopped by your two-room home.

"Mom," I said. "I have the car today. You want to go shopping or something?"

Your eyes brightened—hope shining through. "Would we have time to drive out in the country and see if the watercress has grown?"

"Sure. Let's stop at the grocer and buy food for sandwiches and have a picnic."

Do you remember the day as clearly as I do? You hopped up from your chair and rushed into the kitchen.

"No need. I have the fixings here—boiled eggs, cheese and pork-'n-beans." Your fingers flew in the tiny kitchen and soon we

had sandwiches, deviled eggs, beans, and 7-Up. You snatched an Indian blanket from the cedar chest and we were off.

I drove south to Plattin creek, and there we spread the blanket on gravel. Before feasting we gathered all the fresh watercress we could stuff in a paper bag.

I'll always treasure that glorious day—just you and me together.

Do you remember?

I hear you chuckling. Or is it me? People say we laugh alike. I'm sure we're both thinking of that day years later when you had a bad month—gallbladder attack. The doctor said, "Either an operation or a very strict diet." You chose the diet—with your ninetieth birthday a few days away.

"Don't make me a cake," you told me. "The only cake I'm allowed is angel food and I don't care for it."

I felt sad. No cake meant no candles; and I had so looked forward to ninety colorful candles flickering and glowing as we sang "Happy Birthday, Dear Mom" and watching your shiny face as you attempted to blow them out—every single one.

What to do? My solution? Why am I telling you this? I'm sure you recall. I purchased the largest watermelon I could carry, brought it to your kitchen, and placed it on the table. You watched patiently as I opened a cabinet drawer, found the old ice pick (You know, the one with the green handle that we used for chipping ice years ago when we lived in Arizona and had blocks of ice delivered for our wooden icebox or to make ice cream). With that sturdy ice pick I labored to make ninety holes in the watermelon rind. Do you remember blowing out the candles? It took several tries but you did it. Such a lovely memory and I cherish the photo of that day thirty-five years ago.

I'll place this letter beside the other thirty-one I've written since the day you died—and I'll include the picture of you blowing the fire from the melon.

Do you remember. . .?

Verna Hill Simms is a prolific freelance writer. She joined the Jefferson County Writers Society ten years ago at the age of eighty and is still an active member. She credits them with her writing successes. Verna's stories have been published in two *Cup of Comfort* books and eight other anthologies. She writes for magazines and has a column in the local newspapers, where she shares "short essays on slices of life." She is the author of the novel, *Water Under the Bridge* (Rocking Horse Publishing, 2014) and is working on her autobiography.

Verna's hobbies include swimming, sewing, gardening, and reading. She lives in the Midwest close to her family. She adds, "God has been good to me—giving me a loving husband, and now support and love from my two girls and their families."

4
FINDING THE BLESSINGS IN ALZHEIMER'S
by Kerry Luksic

"The Lord preserves the faithful.... Be strong and take heart, all you who hope in the Lord."
-Psalm 31:23-24

I hated to admit it, but it was true. On many long days, I missed my old life. The fast-paced, carefree fun of my early twenties was gone, now replaced by the slow-moving grind of staying home with young children. After getting married and years in a corporate marketing career, I found myself pregnant with my third child in less than four years. Some days, I couldn't stop myself from thinking, what happened to my old life? Where did all my nice clothes go? How did I come to the point where the only time I could be alone was the one minute it took to go to the bathroom (and technically, it was only partially alone, since my daughters insisted that I kept the door open).

Life revolved around diapers, nap schedules, and managing daily toddler tantrums. Occasionally, I fantasized trading in my overstuffed, Lands' End black diaper bag and weekly trips to Target for my Coach leather briefcase and sales appointments in midtown Manhattan—reminders of the life I'd left behind. Other times, I struggled to accept that the best places to shop were those that offered automatic doors, wide aisles, bathrooms with changing tables, and oversized shopping carts that fit multiple children, their snacks, and whatever was on my list.

I was a full-time mommy—spending all my time with my two little girls, Emma and Carly, living five miles from my childhood home—in the town that I swore was the most boring place on the planet, and the one place in America that I vowed to leave with a one-way ticket after college. But then, that was life. When it came time for my husband, Mark, and me to buy our first home, Middletown, New Jersey, seemed to have the best value—if there was any real housing value in New Jersey. There were good schools for the kids and a great train line for Mark to commute to work in Manhattan. Life had been good to me. I counted my blessings each day—just as my mother taught me to do.

Everything about my amazing mom, Bobbie Lonergan, had changed. This sharp dynamo who raised thirteen kids was showing signs of age, or something. She struggled with forgetfulness and frequently repeated herself in conversation. It was clear to me that these weren't normal "senior moments." As a family, we'd been noticing this for a couple of years. When I finally took Mom to my general practitioner, Dr. Watson barely spent four minutes with her. Mom struggled with a few of the mental assessment questions. Dr. Watson reached for her notepad and wrote a prescription as a preventative measure. She couldn't be sure whether Mom had Alzheimer's disease; but given her age and symptoms, the doctor said the prescription medication couldn't hurt her. The medication, which was designed to temporarily slow down the progression of Alzheimer's, left Mom with the side effects of dizziness and chronic fatigue. After a few weeks, she refused to take it. She had been living independently for years and didn't want anyone to worry about her. But as her daughter, I couldn't ignore what I saw in front of me.

The everyday things that brought Mom years of joy—
sewing, cooking, baking, playing bridge, crossword puzzles—
now brought immense challenges. But she put on a good
act and kept saying, "I'm fine. Everyone just needs to leave
me alone." I couldn't. As time wore on, I refused to pretend
that everything was fine. I knew it wasn't about just getting
older—I thought it was Alzheimer's disease. And I needed
to do something.

Seemingly by happenstance, I came across an adver-
tisement for an Alzheimer's support group at Bayshore Hospital. The following Tuesday evening I sat in a conference
room with harsh fluorescent lighting surrounded by ten other
people. I was the youngest person in the room by at least
twenty-five years. Carol, the support group leader, opened
the meeting with introductions. She was in her late sixties,
with salt-and-pepper short hair and warm brown eyes. She
explained that for nearly eight years she cared for her late
husband with Alzheimer's. Louise spoke next. She looked
about seventy, wore a rose-colored cardigan and khaki pants,
and talked in a defeated, soft voice.

"I had to move Bob to a facility last month. He had
another violent episode. My daughter made me do it. … after
he hit me." She started to cry and Carol passed her a tissue.

Carol explained that, unfortunately, it was common for
a loved one with Alzheimer's to go through a significant
personality shift. She reassured Louise that it was the right
decision and she and Bob would be safer now that he was no
longer living in her home.

"How can I live with myself? He was my husband. I'm
supposed to take care of him," she cried.

Kathy introduced herself next. She was in her mid-fifties
with auburn layered hair and looked exhausted, with dark
circles under her sad, blue eyes.

"My mother tried to cook hamburgers at midnight last

week. I awoke to the smell of burning meat. The kitchen was full of black smoke. I'm lucky the whole house didn't go up in flames. I mean, my God, my daughters were sleeping upstairs. ..." Her voice cracked and the tears started to flow. "We could have died. ... I just don't know what to do."

With each story, I felt my heart beat a little faster. Compared to these people, Mom seemed to be in the high-functioning, early stage of the disease. But is this where she will be one day? When do I need to start worrying about her burning the house down?

Before leaving the meeting, I talked to Carol one-on-one and she gave me the name of a highly recommended geriatric doctor for getting Mom's care on track. The next month I sat with Mom in the office of Dr. Matthew Nelson, an intelligent, soft-spoken bald man, with kind eyes and smooth olive skin. Mom liked him immediately, which was a huge victory since she insisted she didn't need to see a doctor. It all went back to when my father died years earlier when I was a teenager. After watching him suffer and die from cancer, Mom had proclaimed, "When I get older, just take me to the beach and let the tide wash me away." She wanted no part of advanced medicine keeping her alive in her elder years. But Alzheimer's was different—there was no physical pain from grueling chemotherapy and radiation treatments like cancer; there was no tumor to eradicate. And there was no cure. Instead, there were medications to temporarily slow the progression of the disease, which were just Band-Aids to mask the inevitable death of the human brain.

Dr. Nelson engaged Mom in a simple dialogue as a way of assessing her cognitive function.

"So Bobbie, where do you live?"

"Middletown."

"How long have you lived there?"

"A long time. Over forty years."

"Wow. That's a long time. Now tell me, what is today's date?"

"September 17, 2004."

"I've heard you have a lot of children. Can you tell me their names?"

"Sure. There's Mike, Steve, Jim, Cathy...Kevin, Lisa..." After an uncomfortable pause, she let out an anxious sigh. "I know there are some more.....Let's see...Erin, Mary Anne... Joanne, Mark...Leslie...Kerry, and Christa," she said proudly.

"You know, Bobbie, most of my new patients don't have that many children. I think you've set a new record for my office," Dr. Nelson joked.

"I bet I have."

"Tell me about your days. What do you like to do?"

"Oh, I like to do my puzzles, go for my walks, see my children and my grandchildren," she said and smiled back at me.

"What do you like to eat? What did you eat for breakfast today?"

"Breakfast? Well, let's see ... I had a ... one of those things ... it was a ... I'm really not sure."

"Was it a bagel? A bowl of cereal?"

"No, not that. It was one of those ... hmmm ... I have no idea," she replied with a nervous laugh.

"That's OK. Tell me about dinner. What did you cook for dinner last night?"

"Oh ... I know, it was ... it was ...," she said with her voice trailing off. It pained me to see Mom struggle with her memory. I knew that Dr. Nelson was just evaluating her memory, but this innocent conversation was putting Mom through an exhaustive mental exercise. I watched Dr. Nelson scrutinize her responses and jot notes into his file, and I couldn't take it.

I needed to give Mom a lifeline.

"Mom, think about it. Come on, what's in your fridge? Was it pasta? Chicken?" I tried to give her a few clues.

"Maybe spaghetti?" she said without any solid conviction behind her response.

Dr. Nelson made some additional notes in his file and said, "OK, now I'm going to give you a series of commands that I need you to follow. Listen closely."

"OK."

"Put your right arm straight out and then bring it back, grab your left ear, and then touch your nose." Mom hesitated at first, trying to replay the series of Dr. Nelson's commands in her head. She put out her right arm, pulled it back, and grabbed her left ear and paused.

"There was one more thing to do. Oh, I know." She touched her nose.

I flashed her a huge smile. *You did it, Mom! Good job!*

Dr. Nelson reviewed his notes and then addressed my darkest concerns.

"Bobbie, it seems you're having problems with your memory. It could be many things, including Alzheimer's disease. We need to do a few tests in order to have a clear picture of what's going on." He then explained that the diagnosis of Alzheimer's was completed through a process of elimination, meaning we needed to ensure that there were no other factors, such as a brain tumor or ministrokes that were causing Mom's memory problem. He ordered an MRI and blood work and told us to come back once the tests were completed.

I went through the motions of taking Mom to get the MRI to rule out other possible sources of brain damage, while trying to ignore my deep-rooted fears. In the end, the MRI revealed no tumor or damage from ministrokes and Mom's blood work was normal. Through the process of elimination, she was officially diagnosed with "Probable Alzheimer's disease," as Dr. Nelson explained that the only way to get a conclusive diagnosis was through an autopsy. His diagnosis wasn't a surprise to anyone in my family, and it was through this official conversation that we were given a start date to our "long good-bye" and a concrete answer to the nagging question, "What's wrong with Mom?"

With Mom's diagnosis, I forged ahead, plowing into research mode. I couldn't control what was happening to her, but I could educate myself on all the facts of her illness. I spent hours on the Alzheimer's Association website, www.alz.org, reviewing all stages of the disease: its top ten signs, risk factors, and the scientific research behind "plaques and tangles," the prime suspects in killing the nerve cells of the brain.

According to the website, a healthy brain has 100 billion nerve cells (neurons). Each nerve cell connects with many others to form communication networks. Groups of nerve cells have special jobs. Some are involved in thinking, learning. and remembering. Others help us see, hear, and smell. The plaques and tangles could be a normal part of the aging brain. The difference was that someone with Alzheimer's has an excessive amount of them. Plaques are the build-up between nerve cells. They contain deposits of a protein fragment called beta-amyloid. Tangles are the twisted fibers of another protein called tau and form inside the dying brain cells. The plaques and tangles tend to form in a predictable pattern—beginning in areas important in learning and memory—then spread to other regions. The scientific theory was that they work together to somehow block communication among nerve cells and disrupt activities that cells need to survive. My head was spinning with information overload. So this was the technical answer for why Mom can't remember anything? I struggled to digest this information, but couldn't stop thinking about all of Mom's brain cells that were currently under attack and dying off each day.

I read Sue Miller's book, *The Story of My Father*, and cried myself to sleep when I thought of what lay ahead for my mother. Would she get lost driving and wander into a stranger's house or have visual hallucinations, seeing little children everywhere, like Miller's father had?

In processing all of it, I found myself on the verge of tears at random moments while driving in the car, pushing the grocery cart through Shop Rite, or taking a shower. It suddenly hit me—I was grieving over the loss of my mom while she was still alive. I started jumping through the five steps of grief in random directions. Some days, I was in denial thinking that maybe Mom wasn't so bad. Other days, I was angry about Mom's fate and questioning how God could let this happen to her. Sometimes, I felt depressed and alone.

My children started to notice a few changes in their grandma. On the days we stopped over to visit, Emma went straight for the cookie jar located in the corner of the kitchen counter. She took a bite and said, "Grandma, this tastes different." I looked at the beige, rock-like cookies, sampled a bite, and determined that, once again, Mom had left out a crucial ingredient—sugar, butter, or eggs.

"They're fine, Emma," I said, convincing her that for a four-year-old, any kind of cookie was good, even if it was hard and flavorless. I realized that Mom, who used to serve up daily dinner for fifteen people, could no longer follow a recipe. Her famous chocolate chip cookie recipe that she had memorized for decades was too complex. She couldn't keep track of what she had added into the mixing bowl.

Other times, Mom's illness revealed itself when she struggled to tell me a story. Having a conversation with her seemed like a puzzle where I had to fill in every fifth word.

"I was at that place, you know … um … it's that place down by the highway and the people in that big place … you know that area in the back … they were so slow with the meat thing."

I hesitated for a second. What is she trying to tell me? Then it clicked. "Oh, you mean the grocery store—Shop Rite—the deli department?"

"Yes, Shop Rite. The deli; that's it. It took me fifteen minutes to get a pound of cheese." It crushed me to realize that Mom no longer knew the name of Shop Rite, the grocery store where she'd been shopping for forty-five years.

One sunny spring morning, I stopped by Mom's house with Emma and Carly after a short trip to the grocery store. We'd picked up Mom's favorite blueberry muffins; and wanted to drop them off since she was continuing to skip meals each day. There was something about blueberry muffins—she'd eat them any time of the day since they were hard to miss on the kitchen counter. With the muffins, Mom didn't have to open the refrigerator or peruse the pantry to figure out what to eat and there were no instructions to follow. She simply put one on a plate and it was ready.

I pulled into her driveway and saw Mom hard at work weeding her flower garden. She was wearing her standard uniform of Lands' End tan cotton trousers, a navy and white striped polo shirt, and her comfortable white Reebok walking sneakers. Emma and Carly ran over to her and asked, "Can we help too, Grandma?"

"Of course. Come on over here. You can weed right next to me," Mom said as she wiped a small bead of perspiration off her forehead. She loved her grandchildren more than life itself and welcomed them into her daily activities.

After forty-five minutes of weeding, trimming, and my constant reminder, "Girls, don't pick the flowers," we took a break and walked into Mom's kitchen for a snack.

Emma was wearing her favorite pastel-colored, striped dress that was part of her "I only wear dresses" phase and was one of the four clothing items she wore each week. Through all of her outdoor play, she had made a one-inch tear near its hemline. Emma knew all about Mom's sewing talents, that she made all my dresses when I was growing up. As she twirled her long, dark-brown braids around her fingers, she said, "Grandma, can you fix this for me?"

"Oh sure, I can do that right now."

Emma took her dress off, unfazed to be walking around half naked. "Look, Grandma, see my new princess underwear!"

"Aren't they cute!"

Mom went upstairs with the dress to her sewing room, a room she rarely used anymore. After a few minutes, she came down and handed the dress back to Emma and proudly proclaimed, "All fixed." Emma took the dress, examined it, and made a strange look on her face. I looked at the dress and felt like I couldn't breathe. Mom hadn't sewn the dress; she had taped it—with regular household Scotch tape.

"Oh, it's fine, Emma. Look at that, you can fix a tear many different ways," I said in a faked tone of reassurance, while trying to mask the significance of this event. But I felt the lump growing in my throat, and I forced it away. How is it possible that my mother, who has sewn all of the intricate designs of her eight daughters' homecoming, prom, and Easter dresses, is not able to make a simple repair stitch in this little knit dress?

Later that evening, I sat down on my family-room couch, took out my needle and thread, and hand stitched the rip on Emma's dress as tears trickled down my face. Emma's dress was another sign of what was happening to Mom: Alzheimer's, that was slowly stealing her abilities, had now claimed her vast sewing talents.

It was hard to witness Mom's daily struggles. She knew something was wrong, but being a private person, she never talked about it. I was sure she continued to pray her way through her struggles. God was the one constant in her life; and prayer had gotten her through raising so many children and all of the tough times she weathered. As I neared the end of my pregnancy, struggling to manage my two little girls, and dealing with my feelings of maternal incompetence, I looked at Mom and felt completely baffled.

"How'd you do it, Mom?" I asked. Just then Carly pitched a full-fledged, two-year-old tantrum on her family room floor over the fact that her block tower kept falling over.

"I just took one day at a time and, of course, some help from above," she said, pointing her finger to the ceiling and gesturing. That was Mom's lifelong belief—through her powerful faith in God and by simply taking life one day at a time, she could get through anything. She wasn't consumed with worries about the future or at least she never revealed them to me or anyone else. She was a quiet, organized mother who had calmly kept our family running smoothly for decades.

But now with Alzheimer's, our roles were reversing. As her daughter, I needed to help care for Mom yet respect her drive to maintain her independence, even as daily living became harder. It was a constant, delicate balance in terms of how hard to push things with her. If Mom told me she wasn't hungry, could I force her to eat a sandwich? As I watched her weight continue to drop, I knew that I couldn't talk to her like my four-year-old and say, "You're not going to go play outside until you finish your lunch." Yet, she lost twenty pounds in less than a year just by forgetting to eat. Where should I draw the line? As a Band-Aid solution, I purchased Ensure® drinks as meal supplements and encouraged her to eat large bowls of ice cream with my daughters. She was still my mother; I needed to respect her right to say, "I'm not hungry."

The next month I gave birth to my third daughter, Morgan Lynn. Mom was doing only local driving, so my eighteen-year-old niece, Caryn, brought her to the hospital to meet her thirty-first grandchild. Mom loved the tiny babies and as I watched her hold Morgan, I cherished the moment.

"She's beautiful, Kerry," Mom said as her eyes became full of glossy tears. She stared down at Morgan's long black eyelashes, shock of dark hair and rosy lips.

"I know, Mom. She's precious."

Mom kissed Morgan tenderly on the forehead beneath her pink and white striped hospital cap. Morgan was still scrunched up like a typical newborn and refused to open her eyes. But when she suddenly opened them, Mom looked at her in awe and said, "Hello, sweet angel. I'm your grandma."

Time stood still. I watched Mom's face as she held my newborn. She was engrossed with every delicate feature of my baby girl, as if she had fallen in love for the first time. Staring at my mother, I couldn't help but think of the full cycle of life. Here my daughter, Morgan, was just beginning her life, one in which she would build memories, while my mother was fading away from her own life, as her memories were slowly disappearing.

I kept my eyes locked on Mom. Through the years, each time Mom held one of my babies, it showed me the enormous capacity of love she had in her heart. As her twelfth child, I'd always believed that with Mom giving birth to over a dozen babies, she couldn't have possibly thought that the birth of me, her twelfth, was as miraculous as the birth of her firstborn. Yet, as I watched her hold Morgan, I contemplated my own raging post-delivery hor-monal thoughts and knew that I cried the same amount of joyous tears with each of my daughters' arrival into my world. It didn't matter who came first, second, third, or in Mom's case—thirteenth. The truth was that each baby's arrival into the world was an immense blessing. Looking at Mom, I knew that even with the challenges of Alzheimer's, she still had the clarity to experience the love and joy of holding a newborn.

As I continued my journey to accept Mom's illness, I couldn't help but revisit my dark, conflicting emotions of losing my father seventeen years earlier. It had been my faith that allowed me to partially forgive myself for being a horrible teenage daughter as my father was dying and to let go of the entrenched feelings of guilt after cancer had taken him away from our family. I had forced myself to look at the cold facts—I was seventeen when Dad died; it was normal not to like your father at that age.

This time around with Mom, my faith was hitting a roadblock. Instead of the question, "Why is God letting Dad die?" I was hung up on the question of why Mom had to develop Alzheimer's in the first place. I couldn't help but keep a scorecard on the vast acts of kindness she had done throughout her life. She had lived a full life as a servant of God, dedicating herself to her children, the poor, the needy, and the sick. When she was no longer channeling all of her waking hours into hands-on childcare, she put her free time into feeding the hungry, helping out at the church, and counseling pregnant women through the national Birthright organization. I reflected on her infinite capacity for giving and thought how cruel it was that she would end up forgetting all of it. The emotional part of my brain was angry at the lack of justice. What has Mom done to deserve this disease that is robbing her of her memories and her dignity? Have Mom's thousands of prayer vigils been for naught? Has going to church seven days a week for twenty-five years not been enough? Has she cashed in all her prayer chips at God's bank of mercy?

I continued to search for the answers. At first, there weren't any. It took a lot of soul-searching and grieving for what lay ahead for Mom. In the end, the rational part of my brain knew the answer to why this was happening. But it was difficult to admit the easiest answer—it was life, and it wasn't always fair. Through the years, I'd learned that young kids got killed by drunk drivers, cancer struck both the young and the old, not everyone had a healthy child, and just because you were in the third trimester of a normal pregnancy, that didn't mean you couldn't lose the baby. A good friend of mine summed it up as she struggled to accept the chronic, unexplainable illness of her young daughter. She simply said, "Bad things happen to very good people." Horrible things happened all the time in life, and Mom's Alzheimer's disease was just another example.

Eventually, I moved through the sorrowful process of accepting Mom's Alzheimer's disease and came to acknowledge it for what it was. I couldn't stop it, I couldn't control it—I needed to accept it. I learned to rationalize her illness in a lighthearted way. I talked to my sisters and we agreed that at least she wasn't going to suffer the excruciating pain that Dad did. At least she didn't die when I was in high school. At least she had lived a long, healthy life so far, had seen her children get married, and had enjoyed the blessings of thirty-one grandchildren—even if she will forget all of it. I was a Lonergan and if Mom could tell me, she'd expect me to somehow find a "glass half-full" perspective amid her devastating disease. It was how she raised me.

And as the disease evolved from early stage to moderate Alzheimer's, it was true, she had no physical pain. She wasn't on a morphine drip like my father. But she had emotional pain when she couldn't find the right word to get her point across, when she couldn't tell me what she had for breakfast, when she couldn't think of the names of her grandchildren. Everyday living brought challenges for Mom. Yet, she put on such a confident front and happy smile each day. She never talked about how frustrated she felt, but it was clear to see. She threw her hands up in the air with exasperation when her brain couldn't retrieve the right word to complete her sentence or she misplaced her keys—again.

She showed her aggravation as she struggled with small tasks, such as when she made a grilled cheese sandwich, forgot to put the butter on the bread before it went into the pan and burned it, or she left her purse behind at church. In time, Mom occasionally got lost during a short drive to my house or to the grocery store. The disease was progressing. It was frightening for her and my family; but we danced around it, with Mom insisting, "I'm fine. Don't worry about me!"

Mom forgot to eat and take her medications, continued to lose weight, and struggled to pay her bills. After a few months, it became clear that my family needed to intervene. If Mom forgot to eat breakfast and couldn't manage her finances, how could we expect her to live independently? We needed to push back and say, "No, Mom, you're not fine!" We needed to get help for Mom.

Eventually, my sisters Erin, Cathy, and Lisa, and I interviewed several senior home-care agencies and arranged for aides to come each day. The senior aide's job was to assist Mom in her daily living and keep her company. We didn't want to call it babysitting, but essentially that's what we needed. Mom was still physically healthy, and we wanted to ensure that she would remain safe in her own home. We also met with Mary Salerno, an elder law attorney, who drew up the legal documents to transfer control of Mom's financial assets and healthcare decisions, established a family trust, and updated her living will.

Three weeks later, Erin, Cathy, and I drove Mom to Mary's office for an afternoon meeting. We walked into a tiny conference room with a round wooden table and explained everything again to Mom.

"These papers will make sure that no one takes advantage

of you, Mom. It will keep your money safe and your house safe too. OK?" While I said that I was thinking of the horror stories I'd heard of people with Alzheimer's signing their homes over to con artists.

"You need to sign here, right on this line at the X." I handed her the ballpoint pen and showed her exactly where to sign her name. With a defeated look on her face, Mom took the pen and slowly signed her name. Erin and Cathy countersigned the papers underneath her signature. Now Erin would be the primary person managing all of Mom's finances, and Cathy would be the secondary person.

"We're signing these papers to protect you, Mom, because we love you," I reminded her.

Cathy picked up the next stack of papers. "These forms are to help you if you're ever in a hospital. We know you don't like hospitals. We want the doctors to know that you don't want tubes and machines keeping you alive," Cathy said.

"Yes, that's right, no machines or tubes for me. Take me to the beach and let the tide take me away," Mom said and reminded us again of her strong feelings against advanced medical care. Cathy signed the document and became the legal guardian of Mom's health decisions. As a family, we needed to plan for the future, knowing that as Mom's disease progressed, there would come a time when she would no longer be able to speak or coherently express her needs.

It was all so frighteningly simple—within the span of fifteen minutes, my sisters and I had taken control of all of Mom's legal, health, and financial issues. At the same time, it was necessary so that her assets would be protected, and so that no one could take advantage of her failing mind.

It took some time for Mom to get used to the daily senior aides coming in and going out of the house. Sometimes they were a good fit, and sometimes they weren't. Mom wasn't the kind

of senior citizen who wanted to watch TV all day long. She
enjoyed jigsaw puzzles, gardening, and daily walks. She needed
an active companion to keep up with her; luckily, after some
time, we found a few great people to assist her.

Yet, it also seemed that every few months an incident
would happen that caused our family to rethink Mom's care.
One time, Mom attempted to go for a walk by herself without
the aide. Another time, her favorite aide abruptly quit and we
were left scrambling. One day, Cathy showed up at the house
for a surprise visit and found Mom outside in the garden.
The aide was inside watching TV, neglecting Mom. These
incidents raised the question of whether we had the right kind
of support for her. When was the appropriate time to move
towards live-in care?

It also reopened the ongoing debate of whether Mom
should be moved to an assisted-living facility. I stopped at the
local Oakwood Manor Assisted Living Facility for a visit
and had mixed feelings. Marie, one of the front desk residen-
tial coordinators, gave me a cheerful, informative tour. At
a first glance, Oakwood Manor was a lovely place, with its
bright sunny foyer, beautiful flowers, comfortable furniture,
and a dedicated state-of-the-art Alzheimer's Unit to care
for a loved one through the various stages of the disease.
Marie explained how Oakwood Manor embraced the "neighborhood" concept with small, homey rooms and common
areas for activities and dining. Neighborhood Three was
for early, moderate Alzheimer's, where residents could live
fairly independently with support from the staff. Neighborhood Two was designated for Alzheimer's residents who
needed some help with daily living, such as showering and
getting dressed. Finally, there was Neighborhood One, the
area where residents went when they were incontinent, and
often couldn't feed themselves. Marie also explained how the
various neighborhoods incorporated looping hallways that

easily allowed residents to wander while keeping them safe.

As I toured the various neighborhoods and listened to Marie's commentary, it was difficult to picture Mom there. I kept hearing her words in my head, about wanting to stay in her home: "The only way I'm leaving here is feet first." I followed Marie through the hallways of flowered carpeting and into the playrooms stocked with a childlike bed, rocking chairs and dolls and teddy bears that residents could cuddle. I passed two silver-haired elderly ladies clutching their baby dolls wrapped tenderly in pink cotton blankets. They appeared to be friends walking together in their journey of caring for their babies. I saw the music rooms with a piano and CD players for listening to everything from Glenn Miller to Beethoven. Next, I walked into the dining room of Neighborhood One and saw a fragile looking, white-haired woman in a wheelchair, with a faraway dazed look on her face, wearing a large yellow bib, as she was being spoonfed. Her dark brown eyes were completely empty. I thanked Marie for the tour and walked out with a sick feeling in my stomach. When will my mother need to be spoonfed?

As Lonergans, we all looked similar, but we didn't share the same similarity of opinions on many issues, including Mom's future care needs. Some of my siblings thought it was best to move her to an assisted-living facility during the early stages of the disease, while others believed it was best to keep her in her home. After several contentious family meetings and heated arguments, we did the democratic thing and took a vote. The majority of us felt it was better to keep Mom in her own home. Dr. Nelson had repeatedly told us that the optimal environment for Mom was her most familiar surroundings. We agreed that we owed it to her to keep her there as long as we could. That's what she had told us she wanted from the beginning. The few times that I mustered up the courage to even broach the subject of living somewhere else, she vehemently stated, "I'm not going anywhere. I'm going to die in this house!"

Later that summer, Mom started talking about "seeing Grandpa" around the corner during her morning walks. It was the last straw. For a few months we'd been discussing migrating to live-in care and researching various agencies to find the right person to care for Mom. By chance, my sister Leslie was talking to her neighbor and got a personal reference for Lucy, a warm sixty-year-old woman, who cared for her mother with Alzheimer's. Cathy and Erin interviewed Lucy and found her to be kind, trustworthy, and full of love—just like Mom. We knew a live-in caregiver needed to have a good personality fit with Mom. We felt blessed to have gotten a personal reference in making such a huge decision.

When we hired Lucy, we realized there was a lot of work to be done in the house. Erin, the super-organized efficiency dynamo, put together an Excel spreadsheet with prioritized tasks that needed to be completed. On Labor Day weekend, I spent two days helping my siblings Erin, Cathy, Mark, Jim, Steve, and Mike get the house ready. It was crazy to see how much stuff had accumulated through the years as each one of us had moved out. One of the biggest tasks was to clear out Mom's sewing room and transform it into Lucy's bedroom. I felt dazed watching my brothers lug Mom's mammoth, cherrywood sewing desk out of the room. It had been a permanent fixture for nearly thirty years and a physical symbol of Mom's decades of sewing most of our clothes. Now it was being put out to the curb, cast aside—no longer needed. Erin and I boxed up reams of fabric, buttons, zippers, and thread to be donated.

In the back of her sewing closet I stumbled upon a blast from the past, the remnants of the smooth, black-and-white satin fabric that Mom had used to make my senior prom dress. I ran my hands along the silky material and was transported back in time to May 1989, a mere five months after my father died and Mom was helping me zip up the back of my strapless dress. I stepped into my black high heels and Mom helped me clasp my shiny silver necklace around my neck. "You look gorgeous, Kerry," she said. I pictured that beautiful dress, heard my mother's words again, and thought about all the years she spent sewing in this very room, and now, here we were hastily tossing everything aside into cheap cardboard boxes. I felt the first of several steady tears and wiped them away. How have we reached this point with my mother?

With all of the chaos of the house, Mom watched with an anxious look on her face, a look I was used to seeing.

"Mom, we're getting this room ready for your friend, Lucy. She's coming next week to stay with you," I told her once again. "She's very nice, and you'll like her a lot," I added.

"Oh, yes ... Lucy," she said with subtle hesitation. Mom continued to stare at us as her belongings were being packed away and put aside. She clutched her arms around her chest. The noise and activity was causing her stress. I reached over and touched her hand.

"How about we get out of here and take a walk around the block?" I asked.

"Sure."

It was a beautiful September afternoon. The trees were still full of green, hearty leaves, but the grass had become scattered patches of beige, brittle straw, suffering from the previous week's heat wave. We walked to the corner, then Mom turned to me and said with total conviction, "I saw him right over there." She stared into my eyes and gestured toward her neighbor's house. "Right over there."

"Who, Mom?"

"My grandpa."

"Really?"

"Yes. I did. I saw him right over there," she replied with a childlike smile.

I felt my tears start to burn in my eyes and I stopped them cold. This wasn't the time to cry. She needed me to believe in what she had seen, to be in the moment with her—whatever the moment was. I needed to be in her world—wherever her world was. I knew that it was pointless to explain to someone with Alzheimer's the impossibility of their hallucinations or thoughts. It would be ridiculous to remind Mom that her grandfather died years ago and if he were alive he would be about 120 years old—clearly impossible. Instead, I needed to stay with Mom in the world that she was in.

"That's great, Mom. I'm glad you saw him. That must have been nice." I warmly smiled and held her hand.

"Yes, he's wonderful," she said.

"I'm happy for you, Mom. How about we go home now?"

"Yes, let's go home."

It was hard to accept that "Grandpa" was real to Mom. Visual hallucinations were yet one more sign of how things were progressing. It broke my heart all over again to realize that nothing and no one could stop this cruel disease. Alzheimer's was like a runaway train, going full force, without an emergency brake, tearing through my mother's brain, destroying everything in its path, erasing her memories, and robbing her of all her lifetime talents.

Then in mid-September, Lucy moved into our family home. She proved to be an amazing gift to everyone. Mom had consistent quality care and as a family, we had peace of mind that someone was always with her. My family recognized what a blessing it was that we found Lucy when we did. Mom's Alzheimer's disease seemed to accelerate through 2009. During a summer visit, I easily noticed the progression of her disease. In order to take her to the park with my girls, I had to speak to her with the simplest commands. I held her hand, guided her out of her house, and said, "Here Mom, let's get in the car. You can sit right here," as I opened her door, helped her into my minivan and buckled her seatbelt like she was one of my children. It was almost an out-of-body experience when I was going through these actions. I mentally distanced myself during these moments to stop the heartbreaking questions. Could this really be my mother? Has this happened to her or is it all just a horrible nightmare?

Yet, through all of her challenges, Mom still finds joy in the little things of life—playing catch with a bouncy ball with Morgan in her family room, and the tender hugs and kisses from her grandchildren. She enjoys working with my daughters on twenty-four piece, preschool puzzles. It's hard to believe that just a few years ago, we'd sit upstairs in her sunroom and work on five-hundred piece puzzles together.

Mom is still the kind-hearted mother and grandmother who has made a difference to multiple generations of Lonergans. She overcame a difficult childhood; through her faith and resilience, she led an ordinary life, which has now left an extraordinary impact on my entire family. From time to time, I allow myself to have a good hard cry when I think of the life she has led, and where she is now. Every so often I catch myself asking again, "Why does she have this terrible disease, and why is she being robbed of her life, her memories, and now her dignity?" There's never been a clear answer and perhaps, there never will be.

In the end I choose to answer these questions in the way she taught me, the way she'd expect me to—with optimism. The truth is, life isn't fair and growing old isn't fair. I can't be naïve and believe that if she didn't have Alzheimer's she'd be living a pain-free, disease-free healthy lifestyle as a seventy-eight-year-old woman. The reality is that many seventy-eight-year-olds are suffering from end-stage cancer, heart disease, Parkinson's, and other terminal illnesses. Many people don't even reach their seventies—my father died just short of his sixty-fourth birthday. I choose optimism and find comfort in the fact that Mom suffers no physical pain and that her essential core persona—love and a joyful heart—still remain.

Mom isn't violent and she doesn't have to be sedated daily like many people in late stage Alzheimer's disease. At the same time, I don't know if or when this will happen to her. Even though Mom no longer knows who I am, she shows immense delight when I visit her and still recognizes the love between us. This is a blessing within the scope of her illness. I believe it's through Mom's life lessons that I have the strength to accept her fate and the role reversal the disease imposes. Mom's lifelong mantras, "You don't give up, you offer it up; you look at the bright side of life, you put your head down and just keep going" are a constant part of who I am. When that fails, I go back to her two most popular catch phrases: "What doesn't kill you makes you stronger" and "It could always be worse."

It's true that dealing with Mom's Alzheimer's disease hasn't killed me. In fact, it has made me stronger. It has reinvigorated my perspective to appreciate every day, since you never know what lies ahead. It's true that things could be worse with Mom. She could have died years ago or her illness could have progressed at an even faster rate than it has. I know several women who have lost their mothers and it's one of the hardest things to get through in life. The loss of a mother leaves a permanent hole in your heart and can tear families to shreds. Mothers are the glue of most families. Mom is the Lonergan "glue."

Even though my mother has been slipping away for several years, she's the one who keeps my enormous family together. She's "home" for all of my brothers and sisters. Knowing this, I recognize the blessing of Mom being there for me throughout all of the major milestones of my life, from my high school and college graduations, to my wedding, and sharing in the joy of my three daughters. These are precious gifts. I'm a Lonergan and I'm an optimist; that is my mother's legacy to me. Now it is mine to give my daughters.

Kerry Lonergan Luksic is a mother, a writer, and an Alzheimer's advocate. Her work has been published in *The Philadelphia Inquirer, The Star Ledger, The Main Line Times, Parent Guide News, Parents Express,* and *Examiner.com.* Kerry's memoir, *Life Lessons from a Baker's Dozen: 1 Mother, 13 Children, and their Journey to Alzheimer's* was recently published by Unlimited Publishing, LLC. Kerry has an undergraduate degree from Rutgers University and an MBA from Seton Hall University. She is a member of the International Women's Writers Guild and lives in Chester County, Pennsylvania, with her husband and three daughters.

5
BEAUTY FROM BARRENNESS
by Kyleen Stevenson-Braxton

> *"'Sing, barren woman, you who never bore a child; burst into song, shout for joy, you who were never in labor; because more are the children of the desolate woman than of her who has a husband,' says the* LORD*."*
> *-Isaiah 54:1-3*

Loaded with connotation, "barren" provokes images of a childless mother; a wasteland devoid of life; a tree without fruit. For me, the word "barren" reminds me of Worland, Wyoming. I spent my summers there visiting my grandparents. A town nestled between rich farmland and uninhabitable desert, it offers two extremes: field after field of rich, dark green sugar beet plants contrasted by the 'badlands." That's what they call it there—a land devoid of life; barren. The ground is cracked and white with alkaline-encrusted crevices. Nothing grows. And yet, it is still beautiful. The beauty is different than the deep green and dark earth located just the other side of town. It is hard beauty, and to a careful observer—breathtaking. Growing beauty from fertile ground is easy, but when beauty arises out of barrenness—well, now, that is something.

This paradox is not lost on God, master of the universe,

creator of the fertile and the barren. The Bible is full of metaphors of these two extremes. And God is in the business of bringing forth beauty from ashes. Isaiah 54 outlines one such transformation from emptiness to wholeness, captivity to freedom, abandonment to belonging, and barrenness to fertility. *Aguar*, the Hebrew word for barren used in Isaiah 54, means *sterile*. The word has other meanings as well: a desert, closure, constraint, bereaved, miscarry, and useless.

I have wandered in the desert of the aftermath of abortion, been constrained by the terrible grief of barrenness, and felt hamstringed as a mother. But this story is not about the experiences that led to my wounds; it is about the binding up of those wounds. God can bring wholeness out of brokenness; he can restore hope when all seems lost; he can return what has been taken away and fulfill the heart's deepest longings. God sees beauty in the barren and brings forth fertility.

Perhaps more profound than the inability to bear a child is that the word *barren* also refers to a state of the heart and of the spirit—a wasteland of shame, guilt, and shattered dreams as well as the sense of being useless, less than, or constrained. The word *barren* also makes me think of being laid bare, because that is how it felt to honestly face my weaknesses and mistakes. Doing so pushed me into the arms of a loving Father who had the help I needed. And in those arms I found the freedom to bare my soul—the anguish, the hurt, the longing for a filling up of the wasteland that was my heart. And in response to this, my Father came to pour life giving water on my parched soil. As this water slowly filled the cracks and filtered down to the most tender, wounded places of my soul, something began to happen: redemption. Those dry, cracked, barren places began to come alive again with new hopes, new dreams, new purpose. And beauty.

BARRENNESS OF BODY: The Catalyst

The burgundy leather office chair felt stiff to my back. Not designed for comfort, it didn't encourage its guest to lounge. It seemed to say, "Sit, but do not relax; stay but do not linger." In response, I shifted uncomfortably as I waited for the doctor to finish with his patient. Before me sat an imposing cherry desk with patient files piled on one end, and other typical desk items—a pencil holder, notepad, and desk calendar all trimmed in burgundy leather. In the center of everything was one manila file folder, my patient file. The other items on the desk seemed dwarfed by that one, thin file. It had incredible prominence, sitting there, unmoving yet holding essential information about my life.

Behind the desk was another large leather chair that looked appropriate for a tall man; only my doctor was not tall and large—quite the opposite. I wondered how he would look sitting in that huge chair and chuckled to myself. The momentary break from reality that the mental image provided was welcome; I felt nervous, even fearful of what he might have to say to me.

Not wanting to dwell on the forebodings in my heart, I looked up from the back of the ostentatious chair and noticed several framed diplomas announcing to those who waited that he was a credentialed doctor. It was interesting how the eye moved through the room—the large desk, and behind it the grand leather chair, and behind it the diplomas framed in gold which dominated the wall. It had all been carefully designed to make me take this office, this man, and his credentials very seriously. On the walls lining both sides of the desk were shelves holding various medical journals and books, all adding to the professional appearance of the office.

There was whimsy there too—a bit of lightheartedness in

the midst of the weightiness of the office, my patient file, and
the fear that threatened to engulf me. On the sides of the desk
were two glass enclosed display cases boasting several quirky
figurines which depicted an obstetrician holding babies. There
was the doctor slapping a newborn to make him cry and taking
a tiny baby's temperature. The one that held my attention,
however, was the doctor proudly displaying a newborn to his
parents. I smiled to myself again, imagining the day that I
would be the parent getting to see my newborn child for the
first time. Having married only six months ago, my husband
and I were planning to start trying to have children in a few
months.

I formulated conversations in my mind, imagining how
my doctor would tell me the news. It was possible that the
file held good news. The worst-case scenario was that I had
cervical cancer, but my doctor had assured me it would be
easily treated. Most cervical cancers took years to develop, and
since my previous exams had been fine, this would be an early
stage cancer. Or, it could be that it had all been a mistake
and the mass that showed up in the colposcopy was benign. I
wondered why, if the news was good, he had not just called me
on the phone, but perhaps he had wanted to tell me in person.
Either way, good or bad, it wouldn't affect my ability to have
children. I tried hard, once again, to just relax, leaning back in
the stiff leather chair.

"Hello, Kyleen. How are you doing today?" my doctor
asked as he walked through the door, shutting it behind him.
His entrance startled me and I jolted upright in the chair.

My voice caught as I tried to answer him. "OK I guess," I
said, clearing my throat hurriedly. "How are you?"

"Well, not so well. I got your results back, and frankly I
was a little shocked." I took a deep breath and held it, as I
watched him slowly make his way around his enormous desk
to his chair and sit down. He looked down as he walked and

seemed to avoid making eye contact with me. Sitting down at
his desk and without saying anything, he opened the manila
file and pulled out a single, white sheet of paper. He laid it
down and slid it across the desk to me. Breathing out a deep
sigh, I stared at it, hesitating.

"Why don't you read it," he said, not as a question but as
a command.

I wanted to scream, "I don't want to read it!" but instead I
picked it up. It was the lab report from my biopsy and typed
words filled only half the page. I began to read silently and in
the midst of several medical terms my eyes fell on a word that
made me catch my breath. "Carcinoma," I said out loud. "Stage
IV. It's cancer, then, and very advanced?"

"Yes, but that is not what concerns me the most." He
leaned across the desk and pointed to the second paragraph.
"It says right here that the malignant tissue went to the very
edge of the cone biopsy—in other words, we took a conical
shaped piece of tissue out of your cervix and the entire section
of tissue was malignant. At the very edge of that biopsy is a
major blood vessel."

"I don't understand," I said.

"What this means is the cancer cells could have gained
access to your bloodstream and your lymphomatic system. The
survival rate for cervical cancer is nearly ninety percent, but the
survival rate for lymphoma is only fifty percent. I'm afraid the
only treatment option I would recommend is a hysterectomy."

Learning I had cancer was bad enough; I was completely
unprepared to hear that, to survive my cancer, I would have
to give up my ability to ever have children of my own body.
Tears began to fill my eyes, and I felt my face burn as the blood
rushed to my head. My doctor kept talking, trying to convince
me that surviving the cancer was what I needed to focus on.
He shook his head, saying he had never seen a cervical cancer
advance this quickly from the human papiloma virus. I barely

heard him, as his words intermingled with my own thoughts and eventually were drowned out.

How could this be? I was twenty-nine years old. How was I supposed to tell my husband that I had cervical cancer? How was I supposed to tell him that we would never be able to have children together as a result? Anger began to overcome me. My thoughts raged in my mind … this was so unjust, so wrong. How could I have a hysterectomy? I was too young. This was not supposed to happen. I was supposed to get married, get pregnant, have children, and live happily ever after. My Knight in Shining Armor had showed up and I could hardly wait to have children with him. I was ready for my fairy tale—the one I had been dreaming about and practicing for since I was a little girl.

My mind drifted back to playing house with my friends as a young child. The "mommy" character was coveted by all of us. We would set a time limit on how long each of us could be the "mommy" so everybody got a turn. Now, nearing my thirties, my biological clock was clamoring, and I wasn't going to get a turn to be the mommy. I felt cheated, punished.

At the same time, I wondered if I was getting what I deserved for having an abortion at nineteen. The medical professional at Planned Parenthood had told me I would have plenty of time to have children and there was no need to rush into parenting. But my time had run out; I was faced with the horrible, irreversible fact that I had squandered the only chance I would ever have to experience the doctor introducing me to my newborn child.

The cracked, alkaline encrusted landscape of the Wyoming badlands seemed a more appropriate metaphor for my life than Cinderella. My mind drifted back to that horrible day I had discovered I had an unplanned pregnancy. Remembering it like yesterday, I re-experienced all of the panic and fear anew.

BARRENNESS OF SPIRIT: An Abortion Story

I stared at the pregnancy test applicator in disbelief. Head spinning and heart pounding, I stood immobilized by the shock of
a positive reading. I never expected this—pregnant at nineteen
in my freshman year of college. My hands shook as panic
rose in my heart. I dropped the test into the garbage. I was
on my way into the other room before it occurred to me
to hide the applicator so it would not be discovered by my
roommates. Returning to the trash can, I pulled off the lid and
looked in. My positive pregnancy test was in plain sight, resting
awkwardly on the trash underneath and displaying openly the
double pink lines. Grabbing it, I dug down deep into the
tissues, newspaper, end-of-term papers, and coffee grounds,
carefully tunneling with my hand. Holding the loose trash back
from refilling the hole, I buried the pregnancy test applicator.
A metaphor for what would become a lifestyle, the trash can
represented the beginning of the hiding.

The positive pregnancy test resting among discarded rough
drafts for term papers symbolized in microcosm my life at
that moment. Like those pages filled with written words that
were failed attempts to reach that perfect end I desired, the
pregnancy test represented a less-than-perfect future for my
life, and one I was not willing to face. I had a plan. Those
term papers were part of the plan: excel and be somebody;
that pregnancy test and all that it represented didn't fit into
my worldview. And, for the first time in my life, I had a secret
nobody could know because I wanted my life to follow one
course—perfection. The burden of my secret and the threat it
presented to my dreams were almost unbearable. I felt ashamed
and stupid; I felt like a failure.

My mind raced through the ramifications as I barely controlled feelings of panic. If I kept the baby, I would probably
have to drop out of school in shame and disgrace. There was

no way I could be a single mom and stay in college so far from home. I would have to give up all my dreams of being educated and independent. Perhaps more importantly, I would have to disappoint my parents, an unimaginable outcome.

Adoption wasn't an option. It seemed unbearable to spend my life wondering if my child were happy and loved but never knowing for sure. The only form of adoption I knew about was "closed"—where the birth mother never knew the adoptive parents and never heard about her child again. Having an abortion was an option, but it would violate my morals. A new Christian, having begun a relationship with Jesus just two short years ago, I knew abortion was a sin. Marrying my boyfriend and becoming a family was another possibility, but I didn't feel ready for marriage, even though I cared deeply for him.

The thoughts turned over on themselves like tumbleweeds blown by the wind across the badlands of Wyoming, their course chaotic and violent. No choice was a good one, but my need to hide the shame of an unplanned pregnancy and protect my dreams for the future seemed to push me toward abortion.

A DARK DAY

When the time came for my appointment, my boyfriend, his mom, and I drove to the abortion clinic. We chatted in the car about mundane things, nervously avoiding the subject of abortion and our destination. With an unassuming, dark brick exterior, the clinic resembled a doctor's office. The three small narrow windows on the front were darkened, as if to disguise what was inside. I climbed the stairs slowly and paused as I reached for the door. There was no avoiding what was about to happen; the weight of it was as heavy as the thick air.

We walked into a reception area with a patient check-in window to the right. To the left was a room full of women seated on chairs that lined the three remaining walls. I quickly scanned the room. Some of the women sitting in the chairs seemed young, perhaps only thirteen or fourteen years old. Others were older, and I imagined they were mothers waiting for daughters. Most, however, were college age. My boyfriend was the only male there. There were no smiles and no eye contact. The mood was ominous.

The receptionist was pleasant and friendly to me as I checked in. Surprised by the lightness of her demeanor, I wondered why she too wasn't more somber. Had she forgotten where she worked and what they did there? From behind me, I heard my boyfriend's mom greeting another woman and the two nervously exchanging pleasantries.

"What are you doing here?" my boyfriend's mom asked her acquaintance.

"Well ..." she replied, her voice trailing off as if to ask, "isn't that obvious?"

"Yes ... us too." They both nervously laughed again. I didn't look to see whether I knew the woman; I couldn't muster up the courage.

I had barely sat down before my name was called, and I joined the nurse who was standing at the doorway which led to the medical areas of the clinic. As we walked down the hall together, she explained to me that the doctor wanted to speak with me personally. Leading me into his spacious office, she seated me at a chair in front of a large desk. After only a few minutes wait, he came in, walked across the room, and sat down. He seemed friendly and approachable, dressed in street clothes and appearing around fifty years old. He flipped through some papers and confirmed the gestation of my pregnancy. "Are you sure you want to do this?" he asked.

"Yes," I said. "I am not ready for a baby right now. I want to finish college."

He shook his head in agreement, silently confirming my

strongest argument for what I was about to do.

"Does the father know?" he asked.

"Yes," I said. "He is out in the waiting room."

"He's here?" he said, eyebrows raised.

"Yes," I answered.

"So you both agree that this is what you want to do?" he asked.

"Yes," I responded. "I have lots of time to have children."

He nodded in agreement again.

I signed a consent for medical treatment that explained the risks of anesthesia. We did not discuss any other options to abortion or any emotional or psychological risks. Instead, with no discussion about the abortion procedure or how it would take place, I was told I would wake up in a recovery room with something akin to menstrual cramps.

When I came to, I was greeted by a nurse who helped me sit up. My abdomen ached, and I grimaced with pain. The nurse caringly guided me back down onto the table, telling me to take my time. When I was ready, I could get up and leave but there was no hurry. She walked out of the room.

Ignoring the pain, I forced myself to get up off the bed and put on my clothes. I walked myself out of the recovery room to the waiting room where my boyfriend and his mom waited to drive me home. I stayed in bed that day, and by the following day, I went back to my normal life, doing everything I could to forget that horrible day.

BARRENNESS OF HEART: My Search for Peace

The memories overwhelmed me as my mind replayed the discovery of my pregnancy and its eventual outcome in abortion. My doctor had been talking the whole time, but his voice seemed distant, as if it was coming through a tunnel.

"Kyleen?" he questioned, interrupting my memories.

"What? Oh, sorry. I … I was just thinking … trying to process this."

"I understand," he said. "I am so sorry. Look, that is probably enough for today. Let's schedule another appointment and we can talk about your surgery. Can I call someone to come pick you up?"

"No, I can get myself home."

"Are you sure? You've had quite a blow today."

"No, no … I'm OK," my voice cracked as I spoke the last word. I stood and slowly turned. My body felt heavy, as if an invisible weight threatened to crush me into the floor. Silent tears fell as I pulled the heavy office door open. The secretary and nurses stared at me with compassionate eyes as if they knew what news I had just received. They said nothing as I left, but I felt their eyes following me to the building door. The room was silent.

Being diagnosed with cancer tore away all of my defense mechanisms, all of my carefully orchestrated excuses for the choice I had made so many years before. I was angry—at my circumstances, at God, and at myself. I struggled between dread of the cancer and dread of barrenness. I felt pulled by two extremes. Moments of happiness and normalcy would unexpectedly bubble up, but on their heels came the forebodings that I might not be alive in a year. If I did survive, I would never be able to have children of my own body.

The time came to meet the surgeon who would perform the hysterectomy. Having an early morning appointment, my husband and I traveled to Denver, Colorado, the day before and stayed the night in a hotel. I went to sleep that night with fear in my heart, nervous about what I would hear the next day. My surgeon had conferred with her team, pouring over my biopsy results and deciding how best to treat my cancer. Would I have to lose my ovaries as well and be placed upon hormone therapy as a result? How likely was it the cancer had spread to my lymph nodes? These questions made my sleep restless. I lay in bed, awake most of the night, and listened to my husband breathing slowly and rhythmically, wishing I could escape into whatever world his dreams were taking him.

THE DREAM

The calm, sunlit beach beckoned as we walked hand in hand, husband and wife. Lapping waves kissed the sand with the surging and receding tide. The day seemed to hold nothing but promise with miles of deserted beach to explore. But we were unaware of the storm brewing on the horizon as a mighty tidal wave rushed forward, making its way to the shore where we walked. Uneasiness began to settle as my husband sensed something coming. He turned to look at the horizon, and his expression of peace changed to horror. Instead of calm, flat seas, the water bulged up as the wave gained strength and momentum. The water at the shoreline began to recede, sucked into the approaching tsunami. There was no warning, no sirens, and no acknowledgement of the disaster now racing toward the shore at incredible speed. Grabbing my hand and with no explanation, my husband turned to run toward higher ground. Confused and unaware of the approaching wave, my body lurched in resistance as I was pulled along behind him. I turned my head to look behind and saw the wave, now threatening to overwhelm the land and us.

Understanding the imminent danger, I stopped resisting and put my full energy into running, but the speed was too much for me. Tripping on rocks and bushes, I struggled to get my footing. I felt weakened, my energy sapped. Stopping to help me up, my husband continued to encourage me to move forward, all the while aware that the wave had reached the shore and was headed for us. I borrowed my husband's strength as he continued to pull me along behind him. As the wave crashed and began to fill the land with water, it chased us upland. Panic overtook me as I felt the water against my heels and the roar of the wave consumed the silence that had been there before. Falling, getting up, pushing forward, falling again, we struggled to run as fast as we could, knowing the wave was upon us. Exhausted with the effort, we clawed our way up the hill, struggling to get to the highest point on land, still unsure if it would be high enough. Survival instinct took over as adrenaline surged through our bodies. Out of breath we collapsed on the crest of the hill just as the wave surrounded us. Dry and unharmed at the top of the hill, we watched as the water roared past, expelling its energy until none remained.

In the surreal time of a dream, the water receded, and we began to walk back to the beach. Pools of water remained where there had once been an ocean of water. Walking along the beach again we examined the pools. In one of them we noticed something catching the light. Reaching down into the water, my husband pulled from the pool an object wrapped in fabric and burlap. As he began to unwrap it, another layer was revealed. Unwrapping that, he continued to work his way to the center, carefully removing one layer of wrapping at a time. The object grew smaller as the wrapping was discarded. Finally reaching the tender center, the last layer revealed a figurine, beautiful and delicate—a treasure.

TREASURES FROM BROKENNESS

When my husband shared his dream with me the next morning, I was stunned. We had found treasure in the midst of our desperation. Instead of being consumed by the wave and losing our lives, we had been given something different, an object of great worth. I identified with the tidal wave metaphor immediately. Cancer was the tsunami that threatened to consume us. The journey had been exhausting as the shock of my diagnosis brought depression and discouragement. Many times I had willed myself to move forward in hope, standing with strength that had somehow bubbled up from a deep place inside me—a place I didn't know existed. Many times, I had borrowed my husband's strength when the uncertainty of the future overwhelmed me. I had needed him to guide me, to pull me along, because when I looked around and saw my cancer, barrenness, and my abortion, I felt immobilized, unable to move forward in any area. But in the dream, we had survived. We had made it to the top of the hill, and the tsunami had not overwhelmed us. But more than that, there had been hope and even ... blessing. Somehow, I knew that God was promising me his goodness. The unwrapping of the treasure had been a process that took time, but at the end was something priceless. It seemed impossible, and yet I knew in my spirit it was a promise. I found the strength to finally move forward. I had to unwrap all of my pain like my husband had unwrapped the treasure in his dream. I needed to work my way to the tender center, the priceless statue, the treasure at the end of the process.

POST-ABORTION STRESS

In the days following my hysterectomy, we learned that the cancer had not spread to my lymph nodes and as a result, my prognosis was very good, with a ninety-percent survival rate. It seemed the dream was already beginning to come true; with this news, I felt the tsunami waters begin to recede. With renewed strength, I knew I had to face what I had been avoiding for so many years. It was time to deal with my abortion.

I began reading *Her Choice to Heal: Finding Spiritual and Emotional Peace after Abortion* by Sydna Masse and Joan Phillips. As I read, I underlined and circled words and phrases like "moral struggle," "try to block out the whole experience," and "work extremely hard." I thought back to how choosing abortion had violated my own value system, how I had tried to pretend it never happened through secrecy, and how I had pushed myself to get straight As in college to justify my abortion choice. I felt the authors were describing me, and, as I kept reading I came across the typical behavior changes associated with unhealed abortion pain. I saw myself in descriptive words and phrases like "inability to relax," "irritability," "worry about the future," "sexual disturbances," "deterioration of self-concept," and "flashbacks." It both surprised me and brought relief to learn there was a syndrome associated with these emotional and behavior consequences called post-abortion stress.

A DAMAGED MATERNITY

But in all the descriptions that seemed to fit me, I most related to fears about being a bad mother. At a deep level, my choice to have an abortion had given rise to terrible anxiety over the quality of my mothering ability. I questioned whether I could be a good mother because I had chosen to abort my baby. I wondered if God were punishing me with my barrenness. I feared that even God thought I was a bad mother and he had kept me from having another baby as a result.

Complicating my damaged identity as a mother was that I had become a stepmom when I married my husband, just six months before being diagnosed with cancer. Now, less than a year into this new stepmother role, I was faced with trying to parent, when everything I believed about myself told me I was fatally flawed. Already questioning whether I was a good mother, I looked to this eight-year-old boy to affirm me. He was struggling in his role, too, and I was easily hurt by his slowness to accept me. I felt I had to prove myself—indeed, I needed to prove myself to deal with my fears. I struggled between the two extremes of trying really hard to be a "perfect" mother and withdrawing in retreat when my attempts to show love were rejected. Rather than seeing his reaction as a normal response to the confusion of having a new stepparent, I interpreted it as a confirmation of my greatest fears—there was something inherently wrong with me as a mother.

That first Mother's Day was particularly hard. Only three months after cancer surgery, I was still grieving the loss of my fertility and painfully aware of what I had given up when I chose an abortion. That my relationship with my stepson was strained just added to the pain. I was terrified that the dysfunctional relationship we had was going to be my only experience with parenting. I felt confused, bitter, and deeply regretful.

I also felt desperate for another baby. My future as a mother seemed so uncertain. Would I never experience decorating a nursery, rocking my infant to sleep, or hearing squeals of delight and a child's laughter? Would my only experience with parenting be trying to love a stepson who did not want me? Would I always be the outsider, having to watch the relationship my husband had with his son that I so desperately wanted but couldn't achieve? Dealing with infertility, my damaged identity as a mother, and the difficulties of stepparenting compounded my abortion pain. To face my life without ever knowing the love of a child and the love for a child was a fate almost worse than death.

And yet, despite the complexities of my emotions, I knew I had to begin somewhere. Again, educating myself about post-abortion stress helped. I read what experts had to say, those like Dr. Martha Shuping, a psychiatrist and post-abortion healing expert who has concluded that "the source of much of the psychological suffering evidenced in the lives of women who have aborted can be traced to the biologically based attachment processes that occur during pregnancy." According to

Shuping, "the attachment between mother and child begins
almost immediately after conception and the basis of maternal
attachment is both psychological and physical, and this process,
and the natural protective urges of maternal attachment, often
form irrespective of whether the pregnancy was intended or
wanted." It rang true to me that, because the bonding between
mother and child on a biological level is halted in an abortion,
the result can be emotional trauma that occurs on the deep
level of a woman's psyche. It explained to me, at least in part,
why I was suffering so much with these issues of motherhood.

Many of the testimonies in *Forbidden Grief* by Theresa
Burke, founder of the Catholic church's Rachel's Vineyard
Post-Abortion Retreats, seemed right to me as well. One
woman, discussing the way her abortion affected her motherhood, wrote,

> "After my abortion I felt like I was unworthy of mother-
> hood. For years I told myself I didn't want to ever have
> children. When I finally had a baby, I was afraid to touch
> him. I felt like I might hurt him or something. I couldn't
> wait to get back to work. I always considered myself a
> bad mother. I was extremely sensitive to any criticism over
> my mothering. After I finally dealt with my abortion and
> allowed myself to grieve my loss, I was able to reclaim my
> broken maternity."

Feelings of being unworthy or a failure as a mother were
certainly true of me and it helped me to learn they are common
sentiments from the post abortive. I related to the stories of
mothers who described themselves as being overprotective and
fearful or, in the opposite extreme, unable to bond fully with
other children. I wondered if my struggles with my stepson
were related to my abortion. I also related to feeling compelled
to be "perfect," and had felt unworthy when I couldn't meet my
own standards. Some women described parenting as a burden,

lacking joy, and I knew what they were describing. I had labored under the desire to be the "perfect" mother and had felt terrible disillusionment when I discovered my best efforts to love my stepson were not reciprocated. Parenting was a burden for me—a constant reminder of what I wanted but didn't have.

While my own maternal confusion had manifested itself when I learned I would never be able to have a child of my own body and with the onset of becoming a stepparent, I wasn't surprised that for many others it began when they became pregnant again or gave birth to another child. Some women described looking at their existing children differently, as if they were the lucky ones to have not been aborted. Unhealed abortion pain can cause a woman to feel unworthy to be a mother, believe she is a failure as a mother, be anxious over her ability to mother properly, be fearful of being punished for having an abortion, and be constantly saddened by the conflict these feelings create within her. With such emotional turmoil, was it any wonder I struggled with mothering? I felt saddened that many women never understand this dynamic and therefore mother out of brokenness, never really coming to terms with how a previous abortion impacted their identity as a mother.

While I had begun to understand where some of my mothering difficulties came from, I realized I had to face the fact that my need to be affirmed as a mother might never be met through the relationship with my stepson. And while we were a hopeful adoptive couple, I knew it was possible we would not be chosen by a birth mom. I knew I had to try to imagine a future for myself that didn't include the mother/child relationship I had always wanted.

At this time, I found solace in the Bible, especially the story of Hannah in 1 Samuel 1-18. Hannah, like me, was barren. Her husband, Elkanah, loved her deeply and even preferred her over his other wife, but Hannah was so consumed with her grief over her inability to have children, she was unable to see Elkanah's love as a special blessing. Hannah's desperation for a child caused her to grieve constantly over her barrenness. She was inconsolable. In a moment of desperation, she decided to go to the temple of the Lord and ask God to give her a child. Bargaining with God, she vowed that if he would grant her request, she would dedicate the child to his service. After years of sadness over her infertility, Hannah finally experienced relief when she received a blessing from Eli, the priest of the temple. When he asked the Lord to grant her request, she finally found the faith to trust God to meet her deep emotional needs for a child. The Lord granted Hannah's request and in about a year's time, gave her a son who she named Samuel.

Again, as in the descriptions of post-abortive women I had read, I saw myself in Hannah. God had also given me a wonderful, loving husband, but I had allowed the grief over my infertility to blind me to this blessing. I too felt deep sorrow and discontent over my condition. I too had "bargained" with God, asking him for one more chance to prove I could be a good mother. And, like Hannah, my relief came only through faith in God. I began to force myself to open my mind to the possibility that God might choose to meet my need through a career, a ministry, or even spiritual children. I had to trust God with my future, realizing that while it may not look as I imagined, it could still be good. I began to believe what the Bible told me about God, that he "is compassionate and gracious; slow to anger, abounding in love. He will not always accuse, nor will he harbor his anger forever; he does not treat us as our sins deserve or repay us according to our iniquities" (Psalm 103: 8-10). Like Hannah, I had to choose to believe God was good and that he was able to meet my deepest needs.

A LETTER TO HOLLY

As I worked through the maternal guilt I felt for having chosen an abortion and the deep pain my infertility had caused, God continued to nudge me forward in my process of healing. Eventually, I knew I needed to let go of my aborted child—to let her slip from my heart so that I could finally move forward into whatever future God had for me. In order to do that, I needed to name her and do something tangible to let her go.

I determined I would write a letter to my child. When I had a day alone, I grabbed some stationery and trudged to my patio table, fearful of what I was about to do but resolute that it needed to be done. It was a sunny spring day, and I felt the warmth of the sun on my face as I sat down in front of the blank piece of paper, pen in hand. The stationery had a scripture at the top of the page from Psalm 34:3. Written in script, were the sepia-colored words, "O magnify the LORD with me; and let us exalt his name together" (AMPLIFIED). I looked at them a long time, reading the scripture over and over again. Oh, how I wanted to magnify God with my actions rather than hurt him. I bowed my head and prayed, "Lord, help me today. Give me courage. I believe my child is in heaven with you, Father. You know that precious one that I gave up. Father, give me a name … what did you name my child?" Almost immediately, the name "Holly Maria" came to mind. And with that, I began my letter to Holly:

Hello sweet one!

I am your mommy. I am sorry that you do not know me now, but someday, when God calls me home, you and I will get to know one another. I am glad that we will get to see each other as God sees us and that everything will be fully restored in me before I meet you. Please forgive me, my daughter, for not raising you on this Earth. When I was pregnant with you, I was young and scared, and I made the choice not to parent you. If I had known

*then what I know now, I would have made a different choice.
Oh how I have missed raising you! I would have loved to see
your sweet face and to nurse you and hold you and care for you!
I wish I could have been there to hear your first word and to
see you take your first step. God named you Holly which means
"pure spirit" and "holy." He also named you Maria which means
"living fragrance." One thing I never got to say to you, honey,
was "I love you." Please know that I do.*

*Holly, I need to let you go. You are in the care of the best father
ever. I know you are well cared for and that there are no tears
and no sorrow in heaven, where you are. I will return to you
someday and until then, know that I love you dearly. The love
I have for you was created in heaven before time even began. It
is beyond even my own human understanding, because it exists
even though I never knew you!*

*Love,
your mom*

Tears poured down my face as I wrote these words to
my daughter. They were sad tears, but there was something
unexpected in them too—relief. As I wrote, I began to realize
I did know a mother's love. I loved my Holly. I wasn't broken
as a mother. I loved.

REDEMPTION

Now, nearly eight years later, I am the happy mother of two
adopted children. I have known the love of a child, held them
while they slept, watched them take their first steps, and been
able to tell them every day how much I love them. My heart
no longer feels empty, as Holly has taken her place as one
of my dearly loved children. While my relationship with my
stepson was never restored, I am still trusting God for his
plan, believing he brought us all together for a reason. God sat-
isfied my deepest needs and healed my broken maternity. He

brought fruitfulness from the barren. We named our adopted daughter Maria, because she is a "living fragrance" of God's love, mercy, forgiveness, and provision. Then later, we adopted Isaiah whose name means "salvation of the Lord," because God rescued me from death, from barrenness, and from my sin. Indeed, God is the treasure we discovered on the beach that day in my husband's dream. There is none so precious because there is no other who has the power to heal, restore, and bring fruitfulness from the barren.

> "Who is like the LORD our God, the One who sits enthroned on high, who stoops down to look on the heavens and the earth? He raises the poor from the dust and lifts the needy from the ash heap; he seats them with princes, with the princes of their people. He settles the barren woman in her home as a happy mother of children. Praise the LORD" (Psalm 113:5-9).

Kyleen Stevenson-Braxton has an MA in Literature from the University of Wyoming, and a M.Ed. in Secondary English Education from Oklahoma City University. As an undergraduate English major at Oklahoma City University she received the Jean Boyle Award for Excellence in Writing and was named the Most Outstanding Student in the Arts and Sciences Department and presented the Virginia Goff Memorial Award for Outstanding Senior in English (1994).

Kyleen served Care Net Pregnancy Center as Post-Abortion Healing Coordinator 2003-2007. She has led several post-abortion healing groups, given her testimony at numerous churches, and presented a workshop at Ramah International in 2006, on how infertility complicates post-abortion healing.

Kyleen is co-owner of Fashion Crossroads, Inc. a chain of two women's retail clothing stores in Casper, Wyoming (www.fashioncrossroads.org).

Her published writings include "Sing O Barren Woman" in *Deliver Me: Hope, Help, & Healing through True Stories of Unplanned Pregnancy*. Dianne E. Butts, ed. (Connections Press, 2011) and "From Barrenness to Restoration Joy" in *At the Center Magazine* (autumn 2005).

To learn more, visit Kyleen's blog: http://singobarrenwoman.wordpress.com/

6
WHEN I FEEL FORSAKEN
by Catherine Lawton

*"When my father and mother forsake me,
the LORD will take me up."* -Psalm 27:10, NRSV

Mother was my security. She held me, sang to me, cheered me, more than once rescued me. But there were times she wasn't—or couldn't—"be there" for me.

I was a PK (preacher's kid). As pastor's families did in those days—during the 1950s and '60s—we moved often. By the time I was eighteen, Daddy had pastored six different churches and I had gone to eight different schools, from one end of California to the other. I often felt on display as the new girl in school, in the neighborhood, and in the church. Leaving friends and familiar places was always hard, but Mother encouraged me to see new things as an adventure.

"Laugh and the world laughs with you; cry and you cry alone," she'd say, pausing in her work hanging laundry on the line or ironing a dress or baking a cake for a church social. She'd begin singing lines from a gospel song or whistling a happy tune to emphasize her point.

She knew what she was talking about. My mother had experienced some extreme adjustments in her life. When she was a toddler—the youngest in a family of seven children—her mother died of TB. Those were the days of the dust bowl and

Great Depression. Times were hard for poor farmers. Mother's birth father evidently went off looking for work—either in farm labor or carpentry. He left the four children remaining at home, on their own to care for themselves, or to be cared for by the teenaged, married daughters who were themselves no doubt struggling to cope. Little Imogene (who grew up to be my mother) was nearly two years old at the time.

When her school-aged siblings were truant from school, the school nurse went looking for them and found them dirty, hungry, and half sick. She took them to the county courthouse, where they were quickly processed through the system and officially declared "Neglected Children." They became wards of the state of Colorado and were sent, along with many other orphaned, abandoned, unwanted children to the Denver Children's Home, until age twenty-one. Her three school-age siblings then lived at the orphanage (a few years ago the state of Colorado released their records to me). But in the nick of time little Imogene was adopted! The court document has the handwritten words added: "Imogene not sent."

A fine Christian, childless couple was contacted by their family doctor and told about this cute, forlorn little girl who needed a mother and father; needed to be cleaned up and fed and restored to well being; needed proper training.

Little Imogene was too young to understand what happened to her birth mother and why her daddy was gone so much. She must have felt forsaken. But the Lord took her up! The court records indicate that the birth mother had been a church member. I like to think that she knew the Lord and, as she lay dying, she prayed for her baby.

What wonderful people, then, raised my mother (and became my much-loved grandparents). For their adopted daughter they provided training in music, many practical homemaking skills, people skills, and a heritage of faith lived out in daily life and dedicated church involvement.

She was vivacious and talented. As she grew, people said they believed she was called to the ministry. She considered becoming a song evangelist. Then, the summer before her senior year of high school, she met a handsome young "preacher boy" just returned from army service in Korea and pastoring a small church in southeast Colorado. Smitten, they both felt this was God's plan and call. So, a week after Imogene graduated from high school, she married Herbert and became a nineteen-year-old pastor's wife, with all the responsibilities that position entailed. When a baby—that was me making my entrance—came nine months later, Imogene found that life in ministry was not as full of romance and excitement as she had expected. There was a lot of work to do. So, she often let the baby cry and got the work done.

"I've always had a special closeness with your sister," Mother told me when I was a young adult. "I think it is because I breast-fed her. I wish I had nursed you, but I wasn't encouraged to then, and I'd get so busy that many times I just propped the bottle up for you to drink as you lay in your crib."

When they moved from Colorado to southern California for Daddy to get his degree and ministerial education, I was six months old. More stress and busyness came as Mother, whose life had seemed full of promise for her own education, accomplishment, and ministry, found herself living in inconvenient, cramped apartments, making do, working when she could find work, and—having a second baby twelve months after I was born.

Since Mother had an infant in arms when I was barely walking, Daddy would often pick me up and carry me. Then I felt special. I adored my daddy and loved the feeling of being held in his strong arms.

My first clear memory occurred in one of the little apartments we lived in: Mother shushing us with, "Quiet, girls; your daddy is trying to study, and you're making him nervous."

Another time I remember Mother holding me in her lap, rocking and singing the Irish song, "I'll take you home, Kathleen, to where your heart will feel no pain." Her sweet soprano voice entranced me. I remember basking in the unusual one-on-one closeness, and I remember feeling her sadness that she usually didn't let herself show. At some point she made a choice to be cheerful. And she stuffed her feelings, as was common in those days before there was so much pop psychology to tell people differently (even though many people do still stuff those feelings).

When my sister, Beverly, and I were old enough—three and four—to be left in a "nursery school" for the day, Mother got a job and went to work. Always I was being hurried and rushed so they could "get there on time." Then when Daddy graduated and took his first official pastorate, a lady in the church offered to keep us girls during the day. She was nice enough, but distant and cool and left us mostly unsupervised to play with her children and the neighbor kids, who were older than we. One of them had a "Play Doctor" kit, and I remember being fascinated with the toy stethoscope. But then the older kids decided to take our temperatures—rectally—and that led to other things and to a definite sense of being forced to do things—or have things done to me—that I didn't want done. At home I tried to tell Daddy I didn't want to go back there, that I didn't like playing doctor. But I didn't have the words to explain and he didn't seem to understand—just told me I should tell them I don't want to play that game. But those kids were bigger and stronger and knew a lot more than I did. I felt alone and helpless. Forsaken.

A week after moving to Daddy's first pastorate out of college, we were in the process of settling into the small parsonage. On the seventh night in that simple little house, my parents had taken us to campmeeting services and, after getting my sister and me, ages three and four, to bed, they

fell exhausted into their own bed. They woke a few hours
later to the smell of smoke. They jumped out of bed and
rushed into the kitchen and found flames leaping from behind
the refrigerator (caused by faulty wiring). Daddy grabbed the
garden hose but it was hopeless. The fire quickly spread out of
control. As he tried to do what he could, he called to Mother,
"Get the girls!"

We were in the back bedroom. I remember waking to the
sound of my parents yelling and the smell of smoke. Sitting
up beside my sleeping little sister, I felt trapped in that room
with no escape, paralyzed with fear. Mother used to tell later
of finding me sitting up in bed, my brown eyes "wide as
saucers." Mother, who was in her nightgown and hadn't even
had time to grab her bathrobe or eyeglasses, came rushing in
and swooped up Beverly in her arms. Then she grabbed my
hand, and practically dragged me out of the bedroom, through
the short hallway, across the living room, with flames already
burning the walls and smoke filling the room, out the front
door and into the car. It's a vivid memory still. A few seconds
later, as we reached the car, the front door and the entire house
burst into flames and no one could have got out then.

We sat inside the car crying. Blaring sirens grew louder
and nearer. The fire engine pulled up next to the car, and then
there was a lot of commotion. To this day when I hear a siren
I pray for the people who are in an emergency. And to this
day, when I am frightened (which isn't so often anymore), I
smell smoke.

The next day we poked through the ashes looking for
anything to salvage. There wasn't much. The wooden toys
Daddy had made for us were gone. The silverware and stainless
steel pans could be cleaned up. The few items in Mother's
cedar chest were saved. Thankfully, Daddy's books hadn't yet
been unpacked. Still packed in boxes on the outside porch, they
had been saved.

Burned-Out Family Aided
With Furniture, Clothing

Residents of Monrovia and Duarte have opened their hearts to Rev. and Mrs. Herbert Cummings and their two little daughters who lost everything they owned when they escaped in their nightclothes from the burning home at 2047 S. Mountain Ave., Duarte, early yesterday morning.

In response to last night's

where the family is now housed, the church.

Mrs. Mark Mila de la Roca of Duarte, who is heading the aid for the burned out family, this morning reported the following articles donated in response to the Daily News-Post appeal; refrigerator, stove, kitchen table, dishes, Fire King casserole set, dining room chairs and table,

and they will be picked up by the Duarte group. Anyone interested in helping the family may call Mrs. Mila de la Roca, EL. 8-0067; Mrs. Don Blackstock, EL. 8-0066 or Mrs. Harry Arndt, EL. 8-0770.

According to Mrs. Mila de la Roca, the Duarte Community Service Council is outfitting the entire family with shoes and is also making a donation of cash

Catherine (right) and her mother, sister, and father in front of the burned house, posing for newspaper photo and showing new dresses they were given.

Mother grieved the loss of wedding gifts and baby photos; but love gifts poured in from community and nearby churches. The insurance money from the house fire provided funds to build a new church sanctuary. The church grew and thrived and my parents' faith grew.

I was learning that ministry, the church, the Lord's work always came first. No one thought to notice the emotional needs of a quiet, sensitive little girl whose trauma—from walking through a burning house in the middle of the night and barely escaping the flames—wasn't considered or recognized. She didn't know how to describe her emotional needs or get them met in healthy ways. She was expected to be presentable, well-behaved, uncomplaining, cheerful, obedient, helpful. In short, "a good girl."

When Daddy took this first pastorate it was understood that this was a young church plant that had a property with two small houses on it. One house would be the parsonage and the other house would serve as the church building. The fire changed the plans. We both lived in—and had church in—the one house that still stood. Saturdays, then, were hectic, setting up chairs in the living room, classrooms in the bedrooms, cleaning, scrubbing, preparing Sunday school lessons and music, and inviting people to church.

One Saturday night soon after the fire, Mother had spent all day getting everything perfect for church in our house the next day. She was understandably tired. My parents had barely had time to stop and look me full in the eyes. My sister and I had mostly played outside. But now, at bedtime, something started me crying.

I do remember crying myself to sleep sometimes—sometimes crying so hard, feeling panicky but not knowing why, and not being able to stop. Mother—just needing to have the children in bed asleep—would tell me to stop, that I had no reason to cry. She'd give up and go to bed for much-needed rest. Then Daddy would come into the bedroom, after I'd nearly cried myself sick, and he would place his hand on my head and pray for me in his soothing voice. I think that was the only thing that calmed me, and his warm hand on my head provided a physical touch I dearly needed. And since he was God's messenger and praying to God in Jesus' name, I felt in my heart that it was Jesus' hand on my head, the one who I had been taught to think of as my good shepherd.

But God, the Father in heaven, always seemed to be standing at a distance, watching me. I was sure I was never good enough to please him. In Sunday school we sang,

> O, be careful little eyes what you see...
> Little hands what you do...
> Little feet where you go...
> Little mouth what you say...
> Little ears what you hear...
> For the Father up above is looking down in love...

I felt it was all up to me and I was not up to the job. And there were scary, powerful things that could overtake me in dark places.

It was exciting, though, to watch Daddy and the men of the church putting up the new church building. When I attended college in the area fourteen years later, I visited that church, which was full and thriving. I introduced myself, and people told me they still sometimes smelled smoke in the sanctuary built on the ashes of the parsonage, the fire from which my mother rescued me.

With the building completed and the church established, we moved to the next assignment. Because our house had burned down just after we moved into a parsonage, I think somehow in my child's mind I expected some terrible thing to happen when we moved to a new place. No one else seemed to think of it. My parents hustled and bustled around. Then they left us overnight with some church people while they did the moving over the mountain pass known as "the Grapevine" and into California's central valley.

We girls slept that night in a back room that was full of extra stuff the lady of the house stored there. In the dark as my little sister slept, I imagined the various shapes—lamps, figurines, boxes, chairs, dressers—came alive and reached out gnarled, long fingers and claws for me in the darkness. Grotesque shadows danced on the walls, scowling at me. They leapt and licked like flames. They seemed menacing and evil. I was sure I smelled smoke. My heart pounded. I couldn't close my eyes or sleep. I was panicky and scared speechless, but couldn't move. The gyrating, undulating shapes seemed completely real to me. I don't know how I finally slept that night; I can only believe that the Lord took me up in his arms and rescued me from losing my mind.

The new place was a seaside town of sand dunes and sand fleas, but near the gorgeous Monterey Bay. Mother needed a new dress for church but didn't have the money for it. There were some pretty brocade curtains hanging in a bedroom of the parsonage. Mother made herself a beautiful dress with those curtains.

My mother had an older cousin through her adoptive family who moved to California, married a grocer, and enjoyed middle-class prosperity. We would celebrate Christmas with them, enjoy sumptuous feasts, homemade candies, and a glittery tree, with presents. Mother, ever the gregarious person, was happy to have her cousin to talk with and except for keeping us clean and fed, let us play with our boy cousin who was several years older. He also knew a lot more about the world than we did. Once, when I was five or six years old, the adults were visiting—men discussing politics, religion, and fishing; the women chatting as they worked in the kitchen together—they closed us in the bedroom with our cousin to have "quiet time." The linoleum on the floor and spreads on the twin beds sported a cowboy pattern. My sister and I lay on one bed reading our cousin's comic books, something we never had at home. He was on the other bed. Sometimes we had pillow fights. One time he coaxed me to his bed and under the covers with him. Then he taught me some things he knew—about anatomy and how things fit together—that I shouldn't have known about yet. He aroused feelings that I shouldn't have experienced at such a young age. I liked the closeness.

My naive, trusting parents had no idea of this occurrence and other similar ones. But these episodes left me with a strong feeling of shame that grew as I developed and learned more by hearing school friends talking on the playground. This inner shame persisted into my early thirties, long after I was married.

Perhaps the shame was reinforced by the fact that as I neared puberty and my body began to change, my dad no longer picked me up or held me or hugged me.

Thank God, wholesome interests—especially good books, outdoor activities, music study, and school—won in capturing and holding my attention and imagination. Kindergarten brought the stimulation of learning and feeling independent. Sometimes more independence than I was ready for. Since Mother didn't yet drive, and Daddy was busy studying for sermons and calling on parishioners, I usually had to walk home from school by myself. Mother gave me advice the first day. She said, "Don't dawdle along. Come straight home. And don't speak to strangers! Bad men do awful things to little girls."

At that, my eyes probably grew big as saucers again. On my way home that first day I walked fast—except when I saw pretty rocks, then I had to bend over and pick them up; and when I saw carnations blooming in neighbor's front yards I had to linger to smell the spicy scent. The walk seemed long. I watched for "bad men." I wondered, with my five-year-old imagination, what they did to little girls. My Sunday school teacher had said that the very worst thing that could be done to anyone was to be crucified. That's what the bad men did to Jesus. And she said he hung there naked—for all to see! I pictured bad men hanging me on a cross on the street corner, naked for all to see as they passed by. My teacher said that was very shameful, to be naked for all to see. I was already picking up the idea that my body was shameful. It seemed my store of shame was constantly growing.

I probably looked at all men suspiciously and tried to discern whether they were good or bad before I would talk to them. But no bad men ever caught me.

My sister and I loved church. I marveled at my father's preaching; he said more words all in a row than I heard him speak all week. And Mother's piano playing fairly sparkled and roused the lively singing of hymns and gospel songs. I considered it a perfect Sunday if we sang "Holy, Holy, Holy" in church, I played with my friends after the service, and then we ate fried chicken, mashed potatoes and gravy for Sunday dinner. That was the food of heaven, I thought.

Sometimes we two little PKs took our liberties as our parents were busy on the platform and at the piano. Sitting together on a front pew, we'd whisper, then gradually get louder, giggling and poking each other. At those times Daddy would stop his sermon and snap his fingers. There was a moment of heavy silence and we'd straighten up and put our hands on our laps. One time our poking led to an all-out fist fight right on the front pew. That must be the time Mother took us each by the hand and marched us down the aisle and then all the way down the stairs to the church basement. After the service Mother greeted a twinkly-eyed, elderly gentleman.

"Sister C-------, was that a sanctified spanking?"

"Yes, I was righteously indignant!" she replied, always one to come back with a witty reply.

The old man chuckled.

I didn't see the humor in the situation myself.

We moved on, to other churches, other parsonages, other people. There was never a time I didn't believe what my parents said about God, the Bible, about faith and salvation, and living as a Christian. Except, perhaps, the rules. I was too much of a questioner for that. And again, it was more complicated for the pastor's daughters. We couldn't go to certain places or do certain things because someone in the church might see us, someone who thinks going to those places and doing those things would be sinning (bowling, dancing, movies, earrings, lipstick and dyed hair).

We had fun times as a family, my sister and I with neighborhood and church friends; school was mostly positive. We would drive up to the Sierras to cook out, fish, or camp overnight. As serious as life was, our little family would occasionally do silly things and laugh. On hot valley summer evenings we liked to go to the A&W root beer drive-in, where the waitresses brought to our car trays of frosty glass mugs filled with the frothy, sweet liquid. The trays fit on the rolled-down car window. Oh, the delight of that first sip. Then, every time Daddy finished his mug, he'd start burping.

"Well, I drank root beer and burped 7-Up!" he'd exclaim with satisfaction.

"Oh, Herb. You're being a bad influence on the girls!" Mother would chide good-humoredly.

"Hee, hee, hee!" My sister and I giggled with delight in the backseat every time.

But inside I still carried the fear and the shame; and resentment was growing inside me too. I think my resentment was mostly toward the church. But it was almost impossible to separate my parents from the church. The church was often a place of great joy—joyful singing, testimonies, occasional shouts of "hallelujah!" and lives transformed. People caring for each other. But there were those as well who seemed to be "hardened by the preaching of the word." These were critical of the pastoral family, and they seemed to watch for us to make mistakes.

"The problem in the church is carnality," Daddy said to me once, absentmindedly.

The standards in those days for pastor's wives—in the church tradition in which I grew up, anyway—was impossibly high. And Mother was the best! She genuinely loved people, always supported her husband, played piano and organ, sang solos, directed the choir, taught the children, organized the women, had fun with the teenagers, was warm and witty. She felt a little less secure in other areas, but she tried to keep a perfect house and well-behaved children.

"Cathy, you're the oldest," she'd exhort. "Be a good example to your little sister [who is just twelve months younger than I] and watch out for her. And remember, the church people are watching you. They'll judge us by how our children behave."

"But the other kids in the church run around the building too."

"That doesn't matter. You are the pastor's daughter, and you must be an example to the others."

I practically grew up on a church pew, lived in a "fishbowl," and always felt an imaginary pair of eyes behind me, watching my every move.

When I was nine years old my parents gave me my own Bible: beautiful white leather with a zipper and gilded edges. Daddy told me to read from the Bible every night before I went to sleep. He said especially read from the Psalms (conveniently located right in the middle), the Proverbs, and the words printed in red letters, because those were Jesus' very words that he spoke when he walked on earth.

"The Lord knows all about us," he told me. "The words in this Bible are God's words written to us, and he knows exactly what we need. The Lord will speak to you through this Bible, Cathy."

I believed him and to please my father and to try to please God, I became religious about reading a few verses from my Bible before going to sleep. Most of the time, I soon forgot what I had read; but I did develop a habit of Bible reading. I read the Sermon on the Mount over and over, since it was mostly red-letter words; and the teachings of Jesus gradually soaked into my mind and heart.

The parsonage in which we lived at that time was a converted duplex. The dividing walls had been opened up, so it had one very long but narrow living room, a kitchen and bedroom on one side, and two bedrooms on the other side. My little sister got the small room next to our parents' bedroom. I was given the bedroom on the opposite side of the house. My nightmares and paralyzing fears got worse there.

On hot summer nights, in that valley town surrounded by irrigated cotton fields, mosquitoes were a plague. Daddy would come into my bedroom at night and swat mosquitoes so I could sleep and not be eaten alive.

"Cathy, you must have sweet blood," he'd say.

On winter nights my freezing-cold feet kept me awake. Daddy would fill a canning jar with steaming hot water, wrap it in a towel, and place it at my feet. I felt so loved at those times. A hot water bottle on my feet was almost like a warm hug.

One night in that parsonage I was so frightened I thought I couldn't stand it. Some nameless, destroying thing was going to overpower me. I smelled smoke. I was too scared to even call out to my parents asleep on the other side of the house. Then I heard the neighborhood alley cats outside yowling their weird sounds.

"Hallelujah! Hallelujah!" I heard.

That must be angels singing, I thought.

My Sunday school teacher had said that Jesus was going

to come sometime soon—probably in the night when we least expected it—and take us to heaven if we have been good and if we'd asked Jesus to forgive us and wash away our sins. But we would be left behind if we had been sinful and naughty. Well, I had no doubt which camp I was in. I had been to the altar to ask forgiveness for my sins several times; but I kept doing naughty things. I knew I was a sinner. And hell's flames were leaping up at me.

The yowling, unearthly "hallelujahs" continued. Surely the angels were singing because they came for my parents and my sister. But they left me here alone! What would I do?! I stared at the ceiling, my heart pounding. I smelled smoke.

I reached over to the nightstand and picked up my Bible. It fell open to the book of Proverbs. These words caught my attention:

"When thou liest down, thou shalt not be afraid: yea thou shalt lie down, and thy sleep shall be sweet" (Proverbs 3:24, KJV).

I stared at the words with wonderment. I read them again. *God knows I'm afraid.*

At that moment I knew without a doubt that God himself was speaking to me. He understood. He cared. He was there. He came to help even when I could not call out loud or explain my fear in words. He was speaking to me just as Daddy said he would. I lay down under the covers, hugging my Bible close. I envisioned Jesus placing his hand (which was strong and warm like my daddy's) on my head. I did sleep peacefully that night, and never again was so completely paralyzed by seemingly unreasonable and uncontrollable fear. The Lord himself "took me up" and delivered me.

There were normal childhood times when noises scared me. I imagined monsters under the bed. And I did continue to

have not-so-normal, recurring dreams in which I felt helpless.
But never again did that consuming dread overwhelm me.

Now, as an adult, I look back. I see what God did: He
began to transform my imagination. Vivid, real experiences,
dark images, and wild imaginings fed my childish mind. At
night my imagination took over and I expected something
terrible. Then a compassionate God revealed himself to a nine-
year-old. He hung a new picture in my mind's eyes. This
picture was so promising, real, and close that it covered all the
other images on my mind's wall. This picture was so bright
that it outshone the pictures of licking flames and smothering
smoke, of strangers' staring faces and charred toys.

As I continued to read my Bible, over time, little by little,
my mind collected more pictures. I saw myself as a lamb in
Jesus' arms. I saw him sending his angels to watch over me.
I saw him counting the hairs on my head. I saw him taking
me on his lap while all the adults waited. I saw him pointing
out the flowers and birds to me and patiently teaching me
about his Father.

The time soon came to move again. For the first time I
looked forward to the new experience. I began to look back
at the fire as a miraculous time God brought us through.
At the next place we lived—another valley town, this one
surrounded by fruit orchards—my sister and I had good, pro-
gressive schools and many happy hours of playing with the
neighbor girls, swimming on hot summer days, eating fresh-
picked watermelons and juicy peaches.

By the second or third Sunday, though, it was evident that
the promised salary was not forthcoming, as offerings were
"down." Mother rose to the challenge. She pulled out Daddy's
old typewriter and practiced, timing herself until she was back
up to speed, then applied for and got a good office job.

During this time I kept having tonsillitis and strep throat,
so I had to have my tonsils removed. Mother was commuting

daily to a nearby town to work, so Daddy took me to the hospital. I was scared and felt so alone in that big old hospital. I remember "coming to" as I was being wheeled on a gurney down the hall to my room. My throat burned like fire.

"I want my daddy," I whimpered.

"He'll be here soon," said the nurse. "And I'm sure he'll bring you a present!"

Feeling lonely and frightened in the echoing, old hospital with wooden floors, with the woman in the bed next to mine crying out in pain, my throat hurting too much to swallow, I consoled myself by imagining that Daddy might bring me something soft to cuddle. I had seen soft, cuddly stuffed animals through the window of the hospital gift shop. I had long yearned for stuffed animals like other girls kept on their beds, but my parents said they couldn't afford them. Right now I just needed something to hug or cuddle that would comfort me.

Again, I felt forsaken. Daddy did finally come, explaining he'd had to call on some church members who had a crisis arise. I looked but didn't see him holding anything. Out of habit, he stood there jingling his keys in his pocket.

"The nurse said you would bring me a present."

He looked a little bewildered. "I'll bring something next time I come." He patted my head. "Now try to be a good girl and sleep."

He did come back and he cheerfully handed me a little orange bag with a drawstring.

"I got you a bag of used collector's postage stamps. I think you'd enjoy starting a stamp collection. I'll help you with it when you come home. You can learn about them and organize them in a book."

I stared at the bag of postage stamps and must have seemed an ungrateful child. But it wasn't something I could cuddle or at the moment felt I could get any comfort from. I remembered that when my sister was in the hospital for an eye operation, she got a package of farm animals, which she loved and was able to entertain herself with, even as she lay in bed. What could I do with postage stamps?

That evening when Mother came to visit me, she fussed at me to drink something. I said it hurt too much to swallow. She said I was being a baby. Probably so, but I sure would have liked some sympathy.

I got through that operation, though, and was much healthier afterwards. I thrived in sixth grade, got straight As, and was "captain of the patrol."

Soon we moved again, this time to the north coast of California, the beautiful, rugged, remote redwood country. When we pulled up to the parsonage, some church members were there finishing up last-minute touches of cleaning and decorating, ready to help unload our furniture. Inside we found the kitchen cupboards, refrigerator, and freezer stocked with all kinds of food! A loving welcome, a happy start to a great six years in which my sister and I got to attend all of high school in one school and make lasting friendships. We enjoyed our teenage years there, especially the big youth group in the church. We committed our lives to the Lord's service.

That church was able to pay Daddy enough that it wasn't necessary for Mother to work. She was often home, and she enjoyed her girls more as teenagers than as little girls, I think. She was well loved by many people. And people were often in our home. We learned to give ourselves for others. I learned that it's more blessed to give than to receive. I learned that life, family, and church are a mixture of holiness and humanness, blessings and curses, poverty and provision, grief over continual losses but excitement over new adventures. I learned the importance of keeping on and moving forward.

Our parents had a good ministry in that town. I could tell they were happier in this church. Daddy preached with fervor

and even humor, and the people drank it up, responding in
faith and growing in the Lord. Many people experienced spiritual rebirth, restoration, and transformation. Mother enjoyed
directing the choir, entertaining in our home, and singing solos
with conviction and grace. As I sat in church watching her and
listening to her, I felt such warmth. I completely believed what
she sang, and I internalized her faith. I felt the Spirit of God
working through her.

One of her favorite gospel songs was "A Child of the
King." First she'd testify briefly about her adoption. Then, as
she sang these phrases, she'd raise her hand in testimony and
tears would flow down her cheeks (the reason why she always
carried hankies to church):

> *A tent or a cottage, why should I care? They're building a palace*
> *for me over there ... I've been adopted, my name's written down.*
> *I'm heir to a mansion, a robe, and a crown!*
>
> - Harriet E. Buell

Still—as busy as I was with school, youth group activities,
teen romance, music lessons, learning to drive, writing
poetry—perhaps no one saw it, but I still carried hidden shame
and fears from my early childhood experiences. In particular,
I craved my father's attention and affection. In those days,
Mother explained Daddy to me.

"Your father is a very sensitive, loving man," she said. "But
he didn't learn how to express the deep love he feels. He was
not shown outward affection as a child. His father was cruel to
him and made him do the work of a man in the fields on
the farm. From the time he was nine years old, he worked the
large fields with horse and plow. But he could never please
his father, was never good enough, could never make the rows
straight enough. Yet he was always the last one served at the
dinner table, receiving smaller portions than everyone else in

the family, including his four sisters. He was at least once beaten cruelly. His mother, as gentle and beautiful and dear as she was, never held him. Even when he was very small, she didn't take him into her lap or show affection."

I felt sorry for that little boy who became my gentle father. But that understanding or sympathy, when I was in the self-conscious, precarious teen years, didn't take away my own need to feel affection and affirmation from him.

Later, I learned that in our family on my father's side there were repeated, generational sins. There was a tendency to favor one child, nearly always a girl; and a tendency to be unloving and harsh with one child, usually a boy. My great-grandfather, of Scottish descent, left home as a young man to get away from his cruel, alcoholic father who beat him and brought poverty on his large family. Great-grandpa traveled from Missouri to Wyoming to herd cattle so he could earn the money to go back and marry his childhood sweetheart, a Christian girl. They homesteaded in eastern Colorado, arriving there in a covered wagon, and raised their six children with high values, several of them going to college and entering the Christian ministry. But (how could it be?) Great-grandpa is said to have beat my grandfather as a boy, and to send him away from home to live for a time with an aunt. Who knows what happened to him out on those dry plains? But when he himself faced difficulties as a married man with a family of his own, the family "curse" came out through him as well. All his frustrations were taken out on many of his children, especially his one son, the scapegoat who was never good enough.

My father, then, was concerned that he also had a temper. We never saw it full blown, for he sought God's help to take the temper away. And he determined not to be like his father; I think he had a dread of ever being like his father. As a result, he became rather passive. Though he spanked us a few memorable times, he mostly left the parental discipline of us girls to our mother.

Most of the time he was too preoccupied with the needs of the church people and challenges of the pastorate to know what was happening in my life. I recall one time, for instance, when I was a teenager that he and I were alone at home together for several hours. I practiced piano, playing my beautiful classical pieces as perfectly as I could. But he never commented. I combed my hair nice, trying to look pretty. But he didn't look at me or seem to notice. I ached to tell him what was going on in my life, to feel important to the man I so loved and admired. But I know what people mean when they say they feel invisible. When Mother came home, though, Daddy talked and talked with her about the church plans, people's needs and situations.

Mother brightened up her surroundings. I'd wake up in the mornings to her cheery calls, "Rise and shine." She'd be opening curtains to let the light pour in and to help us know the morning was passing and it was past time to get up. I loved hearing her go about the house singing hymns and whistling happy tunes. Listening to those hope-filled sounds was like having warm arms wrapped around me.

We had good family times together, singing family quartet songs together in church; talking together in the kitchen after church on Sunday nights; watching TV programs, such as *Rawhide, Have Gun Will Travel,* and *The Lawrence Welk Show*; taking road trips to visit relatives.

However, I gladly went away to college at eighteen. My parents' expectations were, I think, that I would meet a ministerial student at the Christian college and become a pastor's wife. But I was determined to do no such thing. I did not want that life. At age twenty—halfway through college—I married my high-school sweetheart who was fun and affectionate and a business major. But education, new independence, the love of a husband—those things still didn't take away the feelings of inadequacy and shame festering deep inside me.

As a young married couple, in the town and church where we settled, my husband and I were part of a small group wanting to experience God in a deeper way, seeking to be filled with the Spirit. The Holy Spirit began a deep cleansing, healing work in me at that time. I saw my need to forgive the church and my parents … to give up any resentment I carried. I found a new measure of freedom and joy.

Then, soon after my children were born, my mother got cancer and within a year it spread throughout her body, and at age forty-eight, she died. She was gone from me—way before I was ready to be without her. I was twenty-eight years old and had two toddlers.

Who would want to know all about my daily life? What would I do without Mother's letters—and her prayers! How would I relate to my father without her? Who would rescue me from the emotional fires of life?

So many feelings and questions came flooding in. And it was too late to ask Mother, too late to say, "I love you" or "I'm sorry" or "What should I do?" I would not be able to develop a grown-up friend relationship with my mother, like I saw other young women enjoy with their moms. We had only just begun to develop that kind of relationship.

But Mother's prayers for my sister and me didn't die with her. There is something eternal about heartfelt prayers such as a mother prays for her children.

There were times when I felt Mother close. Often when I played piano or organ for church, it seemed to me I felt Mother's help. My sister said the same about the times she sang solos in church. I thought of the Bible story of Elijah's mantle—and a double portion of his spirit—falling on Elisha.

Songs spoke to me. One particular hymn, *The Church's One Foundation*, had meaning that I had never noticed before:

Yet she on earth hath union
with God, the Three in One,
And mystic, sweet communion with
those whose rest is won.
Oh, happy ones and holy!
Lord, give us grace that we,
Like them, the meek and lowly,
on high may dwell with Thee.

- Samuel J. Stone

This hymn gave me great comfort. Another example of that "mystic, sweet communion" came when I was going through some of Mother's things. One box held snippets of notes, letters, and memorabilia. I picked up a small piece of paper on which was written in Mother's handwriting, "Colossians 2:5." I felt compelled to look up that Bible verse and was filled with a sense of wonder and encouragement as I read:

"For though I am absent from you in body, I am present with you in spirit and delight to see how disciplined you are and how firm your faith in Christ is."

I felt a strong sense that that scrap of paper and that Bible verse were there just for me at that moment. My heart filled with joy.

But other times I felt the finality of death, the complete physical separation. Yes, I felt forsaken.

Then my father, struggling on his own, left the pastorate to go to seminary and study to be a licensed counselor. He began to experience inner healing himself. He wrote to me:

"The most liberating thing I've had happen to me is to take Jesus back in my mind to every incident of hurt I can think of, and forgive in Him that person and let Him have His way in that situation."

He gave me a copy of a book by Ruth Carter Stapleton, *The Experience of Inner Healing*. I spent hours with that book and my Bible, praying and allowing the Holy Spirit to guide me through a process of inner healing of childhood hurts, unmet needs, and traumas. What Ruth said in her book made sense to me. I spent hours on my knees in prayer, recalling scenes of my childhood and inviting Jesus into each scene, each situation. I saw that frightened little girl ... and Jesus weeping with her, placing his warm hand on her head, then lifting her up and taking her in his arms, looking into her eyes, seeing what she was thinking and feeling. He took time to listen to her and smiled at her until she couldn't help but smile also. This inner-healing process helped me release the shame I carried. I experienced a much deeper level of freedom. Recurring nightmares that had plagued me for years—causing me to wake in the night crying tears of fear, horror, and rejection—those nightmares now stopped; their power was broken. A wonderful deliverance!

The healing I received helped me in mothering my children as well ... helped me guard my small children without being overprotective ... helped me with the difficult process of "letting go" of my adolescent children, encouraging their confidence and competence, knowing I couldn't always be there.

At this time I also received from a friend the book *Healing Life's Hurts* by Dennis Linn and Matthew Linn (Paulist Press). The Linns say that the sense that God is present during even the most horrific experiences can be healing. "It's not the hurt itself that causes damage," says Sheila Linn, "it's feeling unloved in the midst of whatever it is that happened. One of our convictions is that the love of God transcends space and time and can go into any moment in the past." The Linns help people find healing of life's hurts by recalling a hurtful experience and bringing God's love into the midst of it through the power of their God-given imagination.

The Lord has been doing that for me in many ways. It is true that for years after my mother died, I grieved and carried a slight sadness about with me all the time. My mother did not know my children, nor they her. I couldn't ask her for advice, or, even more important, depend on her prayers in the challenges of life. I couldn't share my joys and new discoveries with her. I'd never again hear her cheerful voice or see her sparkling, smiling eyes. Who would want to hear my troubles? In many ways, I'd never be able to know my mother as a person. She had always been outgoing, but didn't share her inner thoughts and feelings easily. She herself had been taught not to ever give in to feelings, especially negative ones, not to "wear her feelings on her sleeve" but to "be there" for others.

She wasn't there for us anymore, though. Then my father moved farther away and remarried a woman I had not yet met. I felt more distanced from him than ever. And again, as the scripture says, "The Lord took me up." He gave me spiritual mothers in my church and role models of women in the Bible.

Then one night I dreamed a dream that was more than a dream. It was as real to me as the experiences of yesterday or memories of my childhood. … Mother came to me.

She stood right in front of me. We met face-to-face somewhere in an open but in-between place. Her brown eyes sparkled with pure joy and gazed into my own brown eyes, which were probably wide with wonder. We embraced....a warm, comforting hug. I was wrapped, body and soul, in pure, sweet, peaceful mother love. It was only a moment, but a moment filled with the balm of eternity. It was a moment of total, sublime, undivided attention. I felt unconditional love, both physical and spiritual. Into my senses and soul flowed an assurance that I was wanted and accepted. Into my being flowed a new sense of release, of life. With that hug I knew that I was loved, I was seen, I was known, I was understood, I was remembered and treasured.

It was so very real that it seemed to me the Lord must have allowed Mother to cross the thin veil between heaven and earth to touch me in that way, a way that allowed mother love and God's love to reach as deep as my need. Perhaps she wanted and needed it as much as I did. In that place of rest with Jesus—heaven—she certainly must have gained a new, wider, far more perfect perspective on her earthly life and relationships. Mother love can be that strong, I believe. Maybe I was born before she was ready for motherhood. Maybe the demands of the pastorate, and perhaps even her own unmet needs and stuffed feelings about her early childhood abandonment, made it harder for her to address my needs. But meeting my need—giving me her blessing—was what she wanted to do now, once she was free from the constraints of her earthly life.

That very real, very mystical experience changed me inside. And it lastingly changed me. Who can explain it?

A few years later I bought Michael Card's CD, *poiēma*. In one song, Card sings about his grandfather, who had influenced him greatly but whom he had had little opportunity to know. The following words of the song caught my attention:

"Oh, Grandad, I wish you could be here to tell me what to do
'cause I first saw the light of Christ through you....
And even though we never got to know each other well
I thank the Lord for that one special night
when somewhere between the earth and sky
we silently met, eye to eye
and I got the hug I needed for so long."

- from the song, "For F.F.B." by Michael Card
(used by permission of Word Publishing)

In awe, I listened to the song again. Someone else had had an experience like mine! And he had the courage to tell everyone about it with his song. His words described my experience exactly.

"Thank you, Lord," I prayed, weeping for joy for the way the Lord continues to "take me up" in utter faithfulness.

Catherine Lawton is the author of several books (including *Face to Face: A Novel*) and many published articles, essays, and poems. She and her husband, Larry, are the parents of two grown children and their spouses, and the grandparents of six.

After living most of their lives in northern California, the Lawtons now reside in northern Colorado, where they enjoy worship and fellowship in their local church, gardening, hiking and camping in the Rocky Mountains, travels to the west coast and east coast, and the daily work of Cladach Publishing, their family business. More about Catherine can be found on the web at www.cladach.com/catherine-lawton/

7
FINISHING WELL
by Ellen Cardwell

> *"'For I know the plans I have for you,' declares the*
> LORD, *'plans to prosper you and not to harm you,*
> *plans to give you hope and a future.'"*
>
> *-Jeremiah 29:11*

Looking back, it was all worth it. The disappointments, the inability to relate—even her disdain when I became a Christian—everything worked together for the good. I learned to forgive and let go. Mom (whose name is Mary) learned God is a better God than she imagined.

Though I didn't know it when I was a child, Mary wasn't my real mom. When my real mom was alive, before I was born, Mary had been her neighbor and close friend. My real mom, Ellen, once told my dad, "If anything happens to me, I want Mary to have the children." Mary had lost her only son in a drowning accident years earlier and yearned for a family of her own.

Did Ellen, my real mom, have a premonition she would die young? No one knows for sure, but that's exactly what happened. Did Mary get the children? Yes, eventually she did; and this is how it all came about.

One Sunday afternoon when my mother was full term with me, my folks took my sister for a stroll. Suddenly, without warning, my mom collapsed. She was rushed to the hospital, but the doctor, a family friend, wasn't able to save her. My mom died that day from a massive stroke.

Dr. McIvor took me by C-section in hopes of rescuing me. He administered mouth-to-mouth resuscitation, a practice not widely accepted yet in those days, even when it seemed I had given up and slipped away. He refused to quit. For twenty minutes he continued—he couldn't face Dad with the news that both his wife and their child had died. I was officially born when I began to breathe on my own. When Dad heard the news, he replied "It's like a miracle"—surprising words coming from an agnostic.

In those days, the child usually died with the mother. The event was extraordinary and, therefore, newsworthy. *The Oakland Tribune* carried the story on the front page alongside a picture of a pretty nurse holding me, all wrapped up, squashed head peeking out.[1] It gave the doctor credibility among his colleagues and a short-lived celebrity at the same time.

The event of my birth wasn't only rare; it was controversial. A segment of the *Tribune* called Vox Populi published letters to the editor. Many readers responded to the human interest story enthusiastically; some did not. One negative note suggested I wasn't supposed to live, charging interference with nature. Others pitied the poor child bereft of a mother's love and care. They had no way of knowing God would provide a stepmother for my sister and me when Dad remarried two years later. He married the neighbor, Mary.

Until then our Aunt Esther took care of my sister and me. We lived with my aunt and uncle while Dad commuted to work at Grand Coulee Dam in Washington state. We played with our teenage cousins, whose patience with us was admirable. Home movies show me chasing more balls than catching them. Mostly I watched them play while bouncing up and down in my jumper chair.

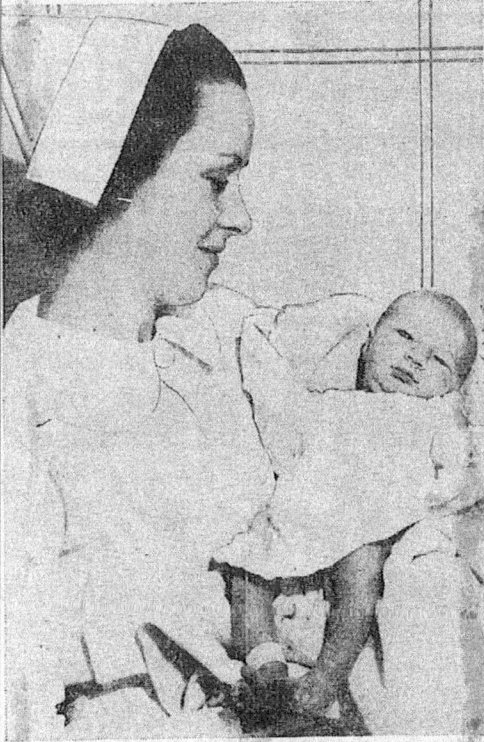

DEATH WAS CHEATED

Miss **Mary Flaherty Flaherty**, student nurse at Providence Hospital, holding **Ellen Marie Lewis**, who was brought into the world through a surgeon's skill 11 minutes after the death of her mother. The child, now three days old, weighed over seven pounds at birth, and is "doing fine."—*Tribune photo.*

Newspaper clipping from Oakland Tribune
story with picture of newborn Ellen

One day my aunt coached me to say, "I want to stay with Onne (as I called her)." She knew Dad and my new mom were coming to take us home with them. When Mother reached down to pick me up, I repeated my lines. She asked me if Onne had told me to say that, and, of course, I told the truth. She scolded Aunt Esther for putting me up to it. Other than that one incident, I don't recall the separation being a particularly emotional or traumatic experience.

My new mom was a beautiful woman with dark auburn hair and green eyes. She was blessed with generous curves on her medium build. She was raised on a farm in the Midwest, the older sister to two brothers. Her nurturing experience prepared her to care for us as well as anyone could.

Our family lived in the Richmond District of San Francisco most of our lives, first in a rental house, then in one Mom and Dad were able to purchase from a local builder, Henry Dolger. Mr. Dolger said, "You look like honest people" and agreed to sell it to them with a handshake. My, how times have changed!

We were happy there, attending Lafayette Grammar School, playing with neighbor children, learning the piano. As we grew more responsible, we were allowed to walk to the local playground. I joined a Brownie troop and my sister became a Bluebird. My troop sold Girl Scout cookies, earned badges, and took field trips. When I graduated to Girl Scouts, I was able to go to camp, my first experience surrounded by nature. I loved it. It was a side of life to which I wasn't exposed, living in the city.

Occasionally, Mom acted as buffer between Dad's strict discipline and our sensitivity. She usually deferred to Dad's wishes, however. Dad was a self-made man, who through education and hard work had raised himself from poverty to a solid middle-class career. Later, though, when Dad began his job as a city official, Mom began to be uncomfortable and experience insecurity. Dad asked her to read a novel about political intrigue. After reading the novel, she commented, "I wish I'd never read that book. It's scary what happens in politics."

With Dad's new status in life, the little two-bedroom house was no longer appropriate for one in his position. So Mom began looking around the neighborhood for another home; and one day after church we went "'splorin." We checked out an older three-story home (two stories above a garage) in a location only one block from our grammar school.

Dad looked at it, and agreed it was appropriate for their new lifestyle. Mom liked the fog that rolled in from the nearby beach, preceded by moaning foghorns.

I was in the fifth grade when we moved. I missed playing with the kids on the old block. The only two children in the new neighborhood were two uninteresting boys.

Our lifestyle was more formal in our new location. For instance, Mom said, "Don't bring anyone home without asking first." Since that wasn't possible, it put an end to friendly spontaneity. Whereas many parents don't want their children going to other people's houses and prefer they have their friends over instead, ours was the opposite situation. From then on I had one best friend and my sister for company.

Mom was skilled at sewing, crocheting, and needlepoint. Whenever she had free time, she could be found in her favorite chair, her current needlework project in her lap. Mom crocheted a tablecloth that fit the dining room table when all three leaves were in it. It took years to accomplish, but she never seemed to tire of working on it.

When that goal was accomplished, she made needlepoint seat covers for the dining room chairs. More needlepoint became pillows with velvet backing. Two designs, using yarns in the living room's colors, were framed as pictures. She was always working to make our home more beautiful.

Mom was also a marvelous cook. She'd developed the skill growing up on the farm, helping cook for the family and hired hands. They needed hearty meals to do heavy farm work, and they needed quantity too. I used to marvel at her ability to get several dishes ready all at the same time.

I remember her pies most of all—especially lemon meringue. When I was old enough to help in the kitchen, I watched her make it. She began with the pie crust. There was no recipe. It was "a little bit of this and a little bit of that" and lots of experience. She just knew when it was right.

The lemon filling, however, was written on a recipe card which Mom followed exactly. One item not on the recipe, but added to almost anything she cooked, was a walnut-sized chunk of butter. "Everything tastes better with butter," she'd say.

Another wonderful creation was her apple pie. Every August we drove north to Sebastopol, famous for its Graven-stein apples. We went to Mrs. Beatty's orchard and gathered apples that had fallen from the trees to the soft soil below. We left the blemished ones behind, but filled several lugs to the top with the good ones, then filled the trunk with the lugs. The fruity aroma as we drove home promised bubbling pies at their golden best. We were never disappointed.

Many apples became applesauce which was then canned. My sister and I would compete with Mom to see who could peel an apple without breaking the skin. Mom always ended with a long coil of shiny green peel with barely any white pulp attached. We, if we were lucky, might be able to do it, but only if we took thick pieces of apple along with it. Nowadays people buy apple peelers to perform the task. Where's the skill in that?

Mom canned steadily throughout the summer months. We would go to the farmer's market south of the city to buy the produce. She would walk around, and with a trained eye, pick out the best quality peaches, tomatoes, and pickling cucumbers. Once they were brought into the house, Mary and I helped Mom under her direction.

First, we boiled the jars and rings. When they'd been in the water long enough to be sanitized, we lifted them out onto freshly washed towels to let them drain. Like a team on an assembly line, we worked in earnest, peeling, pitting, and peeling some more. The canned fruit was left to cool until the lids sucked inward, creating a seal. After that, some of them went into the cooler on the back porch and the rest down to the storage room in the basement.

Mom's pickles were legendary. She made them by herself, combining exact proportions of dill weed, salt, pickling spice, and vinegar to achieve perfection. She only canned a few jars of pickles, so it was a special occasion when we brought one up from the basement. Opening a jar of her pickles was a ceremony. First the rusty ring was discarded, the lid opened with a whoosh. When the dill weed and garlic were removed, the first pickle was taken out and fingered for texture. They were perfectly crisp because they never lasted long enough to get soft. Aunt Emma, Mom's best friend, insisted on having a dill pickle with her apple pie. She made wonderful dills too.

Mom gave us years of love and care, kept a good home for us, and instilled the discipline we needed. Only later did we become aware of her shortcomings and enlarge them in our minds to the point they overshadowed the good. Disillusionment and disappointment increased as we gained a more realistic view of our parents.

One day coming back from camp, I looked out the car window to see my folks waiting for me. It was a strange scene and an unsettling one, because Mom looked like a different person. She was standing as if at attention in an unflattering black suit and white blouse, wearing an equally unflattering hat. She was wearing black "nurses'-bunion shoes" and wasn't wearing her customary smile. Something must have happened while I was away at camp, but we never discussed it and I never found out.

Parents didn't communicate with their children in those days. To do that would have made us equals. Instead, they led, they taught, they lectured, they gave orders, and made pronouncements. They didn't lose their tempers, raise their voices, or admit weakness. It was all about self control and keeping the upper hand. And it was unreal.

For example, a friend of mine was living with us for a while. She was running a bath and got distracted. Mom saw water dripping through the ceiling and said in her normal tone of voice, "Is someone running the water?" My reaction was totally different. I bounded up the stairs yelling, "Delores, the tub is running over." To this day, I cannot even pretend I should have behaved like Mom.

It was too bad Dad and Mom never talked with us—to us, yes, but not with us. There's so much wisdom and knowledge they could have passed along that we could have used in our lives. But they were doing what they thought was best.

When I was a child, I trusted my parents and put them on a pedestal. I believed they were telling me the truth because they insisted I should. But as I grew more detached in my teen years, I began to notice inconsistencies, especially in Mom's stories. Onne told me things about her I didn't know before, maybe out of the wrong motivation, but factual, nevertheless.

The biggest shock came when a neighbor dropped in while the folks were gone. He'd been walking his dog and probably planned to have a drink with Dad, as was their custom. He'd already been drinking enough to loosen his tongue and good sense. While we attempted to entertain him, he told my sister and me, "You know, your mom is not your real mother." He rattled on and on, but I couldn't tell you another word he said. I was in shock! Suddenly my foundation was shaken as if the ground were liquefying under me. All sorts of thoughts were racing through my head.

"What else hasn't she told me? Why did Dad agree to this subterfuge? How can I believe anything else she's told me?" My questions kept coming, and I didn't know the answers.

My sister wasn't nearly affected as I was. She'd already begun to lose respect for Mom, who now looked matronly, while she herself was becoming interested in fashion and personal appearance. Mary, in fact, looked like the young Elizabeth Taylor. She was embarrassed that Mom still kept sewing dresses for herself, even after she could afford to purchase nicer clothes. Mom should have upgraded her wardrobe along with Dad's promotion, but maybe she didn't know how.

When the folks returned, we told them what Ralph had said. They were annoyed at him, and made vague attempts to explain why they had kept the facts hidden. But their reasons weren't satisfactory enough to put me at ease. Perhaps if they had inquired how we felt about it or explained their viewpoint, I could have understood it better. But they didn't. My emotions were in chaos.

Left alone to deal with the news, I didn't handle it very well. In spite of our family nominally attending church, I had very little Christian training, or I would have known to forgive Mom on the spot. Instead, I was unmerciful and condemned her. In my mind, she was no longer trustworthy.

Little memories that hadn't made sense at the time, now had meaning. When as a child I grabbed Dad's legs while Mom was hugging him, she said, "How long will Ellen come between us?"

"Ellen isn't coming between us," he growled. I didn't understand why he said that, because *I was* standing right there between them.

Another time, when the family had gone to see the movie *Song of Bernadette*, Dad asked my sister if she believed in miracles. She said no. Then he asked me, and I said yes. He softly whispered, "So did your mother." I didn't know why he said that. Mom was right there with us, and he hadn't asked her.

One Christmas I asked the folks why "Uncle" Norman (my birth mother's brother) and "Auntie" Froines always came over and brought presents for Mary and me. "We don't see them any other time of the year," I observed. They never came again, so we were cut off from that side of our family. It's reasonable to assume the folks asked them not to come back.

At the dinner table during a discussion of food values, Dad said "As soon as your mother was pregnant, she began studying nutrition."

Mom piped up defensively, "So did I." That just didn't make sense. I think Dad had been leaving hints about our mother for some time.

Dad had worked hard as a young man to rise above his poor "white trash" beginnings. He studied constantly, always improving himself. He worked days and studied nights, moving up in whatever position he held. Eventually, he became a CPA and went into business for himself. My real mom had helped out at the office. They were true partners in every way.

After Ellen passed away and Dad remarried, he took the civil service test to become administrative assistant to the mayor. He tested highest, so he was awarded the job—a position he held for many years. His main responsibility was managing San Francisco's budget. Keeping the budget balanced wasn't easy, given the demands from various interest groups and working with the supervisors.

When Mayor Lapham appointed him manager of the Recreation and Parks Department, Dad called it "The best job in the city." It was the last job he held.

He could have had a position in the Federal Bureau of the Budget, but was turned down, not for any fault of his own. But

Mom had been vetted, too, and in the process it was discovered she'd been jailed for shoplifting. Dad was furious that she had kept that fact from him.

Dad asked my sister and me what we thought. Should he divorce Mom? I said "No, we love her." Mary shushed me up. She was aware we could have a better social position if he did. Even the suggestion of a divorce is unnerving to a child. But nothing more was said about the possibility.

Mom quietly asked me, "Can you understand why I would do such a thing? It was Billy's—her son's—birthday and I couldn't afford to buy him a present." I told her I understood, and maybe that helped her somehow. Mom had a tender heart that sometimes got her into trouble.

One day she asked us girls if we would mind if her brother Chet came to live with us. He had no place to go since he'd retired from the Navy. Dad agreed to let him come on a temporary basis. Uncle Chet was an alcoholic and begged Mom to buy him something to drink day after day until she gave in. One night he fell asleep with a lighted cigarette and set the bed on fire. The fire department pulled the mattress out into the street, and there our family stood in robes and slippers while the firemen made sure it was safe to go back in. Dad told Chet to leave and never come back.

Other resentments toward Mom piled up. I seemed to have promise as an artist, and my teacher showed a particular drawing to someone who recommended I take private classes at the Legion of Honor Museum, which was near our home. For some reason, I wasn't allowed to do it, and missed out on the enrichment and self esteem that could come from using one's gifts.

Then, if either parent had picked up on it, they would have known I loved to sing. Mom would only correct me: "We don't sing at the table." And I used to sing along while playing the piano. At a piano recital we sang Christmas carols. The woman in front of us urged Mom to give me singing lessons, that I had a gift. But when I wanted to join the chorus in school, she insisted I take violin lessons instead. I overheard her tell Dad "She likes to sing, but she'll never amount to anything." Years later, I discovered I had all the aptitudes to be an outstanding soloist.

Mom had gifts at which she excelled; but she didn't appreciate mine. She wanted me to stick with piano. (Later I learned my real mother had been an accomplished pianist.) My sister had a touch I didn't have. As hard as I tried, she was always much better. Piano was right for her, but not for me.

Mom emphasized the importance of keeping a promise, but didn't always follow her own advice. In a couple of cases she gave away things that she had promised to me.

One was a necklace of iridescent crystal balls. I loved the colors floating on the invisible surfaces. Mom promised she would give them to me, but they were so fragile, I knew I couldn't have them till I was much older. Every once in a while I'd go look at them in her jewelry box. One day, to my horror, they were gone. She said she didn't remember what happened to them. I didn't believe her; how could she forget? I grieved over their loss. Mom didn't even apologize. In my eyes, she was a hypocrite.

She also promised to make me a dress from some beautiful blue fabric that faded into pink and back. One day I came home just as she was fitting Mary with a dress made from that fabric. "You promised I could have that," I protested. She mumbled something in return that wasn't even a decent excuse. It just added to my censorious attitude toward her. I was developing a bitterness that took a long time and God's help to eliminate from my life.

I believe God sent me an ambassador in the person of Delores. She followed God's lead to move from Detroit to the San Francisco Bay Area and started attending our little neighborhood church. That's where I met her, and we soon became friends. She'd previously heard of an outstanding church and pastor in Berkeley, across the bay. One of the women at Lincoln Park Presbyterian Church mentioned that her brother attended the Berkeley church. Delores wanted to visit there and made contact with Don to get some information. We did go visit, and I was so impressed I thought, "This is real Christianity." I was so green in spiritual matters, I didn't know differences existed within the same denomination.

This was not like the church we attended as a family. We would go on Sunday, but it had no application to our lives the rest of the week. It was just the right thing to do. I don't recall ever hearing the gospel. However, I heard that Jesus loves me from our Sunday school teacher, and that truth has always stayed with me. For that I'm grateful.

There was a large singles' group at the Berkeley church. The people there talked about God as if they knew him and he was active in their lives. Delores talked about the Lord, too, and I found that very appealing. I also knew I didn't have what they had—a real relationship with Jesus.

We began attending First Presbyterian Church on a regular basis. We went to the singles' group at night and then stayed for the evening service. The first time I heard Dr. Munger preach the gospel, I went forward. I really had no idea what I'd done, but with the help of Bible studies, mature Christian friends, and caring pastors, I began to grow.

When I returned home from a weekend conference, I told Mom I had committed my life to Christ and wanted him to be Lord of my life. Thinking she would be pleased, I was totally unprepared for her reaction. I'd never seen her so angry.

"We raised you girls to be wives of executives," she hissed. In her mind, she didn't think you could be both.

"I was afraid this would happen," Dad responded when he heard the news. He thought Mom had a tendency in that direction because she was president of the Women's Association. But now it was obvious, holding that position was not motivated by piety.

I was so unprepared for their attacks, I experienced psychological pain the likes of which I've never had since. I was torn wide open, unprotected and totally vulnerable. But I wasn't going to deny the Lord. I retreated like a wounded animal, terrified of speaking up again.

I made an effort not to rattle the folks' boat, but I continued reading my Bible when I was alone. It was gradually recycling my secular mind and putting steel in my spine. If Mom walked in on me while I was reading, she'd scoff, "Put that down and get to work."

One day at the dinner table, I said something about the Lord, and she commented, "Only people in insane asylums talk about Jesus." So I lived like a closet Christian until Delores moved in with us.

Delores was a nurse and usually worked the midnight shift. She needed the extra money it provided because she was single, and living in the city was very expensive compared to the Midwest. It wasn't long before she asked if she could stay with us. Mom was glad to have the money.

Delores was an established Christian and helped me see the situation at home for what it was. She could see it would be better for me to move out and get a place of my own. I was not sure what to do, so I talked to Dr. Munger about it. After hearing all the details, he agreed that it would be better if I did move.

Combining what I gave Mom and what Delores paid her, we had enough to get a nice apartment, especially if we were to move to Berkeley. When I told Mom our plan, she said she didn't believe that was a good idea. When I said Dr. Munger suggested I do it, she gave me a stone-faced look, but said nothing.

Moving to Berkeley freed us up to dive into church activities and the pool in the apartment complex. Delores and I could have friends over, and we could visit them. It was lots of fun, and we showed up at church every time the doors opened. It was a concentrated time of spiritual growth.

Because I was raised with a secular mindset and encouraged to be independent, the Holy Spirit had much recycling to do within me. But I never felt God was impatient with me. After I understood salvation well enough, I wanted my family to know how good God is too. But I didn't have faith to believe for them, so I kept in touch with them on good terms as much as possible.

When the Billy Graham Crusade was preparing to come to the Cow Palace in San Francisco, they contacted Bay Area churches for volunteers to serve as counselors to the people who came forward to receive Christ. I passed their test and was accepted. This was my first experience with ministry.

My good friend, Don, was going to counsel too. We wound up riding back and forth to the city together, talking of serving the Lord and other ministries. As it turned out, we became more than friends and eventually were married.

Don had been raised in a Christian home and his personality reflected it. I learned so much from him. Marriage is challenging, and we were totally different people—different in expectations and different in backgrounds. God helped us smooth down the rough edges and learn to work in harmony.

I began to see myself in the mirror of the Scriptures. I was judgmental, unforgiving, and self-righteous, especially in relationship to Mom. I lacked compassion, was self-centered and selfish. When I finally understood I wouldn't be forgiven unless I forgave her, I found the motivation to rid myself of unforgiveness.

What a task! Every thought of her, I had to forgive her. Every word about her couldn't sound bitter. I knew I had to forgive her from my heart, and I needed help doing that.

A teacher explained that forgiveness is like a bell. Picture the Liberty Bell in your mind. The bell swings wide and you hear a loud ring. The ring brings to mind the incident that's causing you pain. You, by an act of your will—not feelings, choose to forgive that person. The bell swings back.

The bell doesn't swing as far the next time. The ring isn't quite so loud either. You choose to forgive again. And as the bell swings more and more slowly, the ring grows softer and softer. And it's easier to forgive every time. Finally, the sting from what happened originally is diminished, if not forgotten.

Don and I worked at our relationships with Mom and Dad too. We did our best to be there for them, especially when Dad had a stroke. Mom was his caregiver for seven years until he passed away. I had lost my dad gradually because he was less and less the person I knew. Other of Mom's friends moved in with her, one after another dying there.

One day there was a breakthrough. I was over at Mom's house with our teenage son and his friend. Mom was amused at Ken's teasing and Lisa's giggles. She put down her cup, looked me in the eye, and admitted, "Well, it's worked out all right. I guess you did the right thing. I thought I was doing the right thing—"

By then I was at her side reassuring her she had done well, but that she needed to take it a step farther. With her heart wide open, I took her hand in mine and we prayed together while she received Christ into her life and the salvation he brought with him.

I quickly brought her a more contemporary translation of the Bible than the one she had. We lived too far away to supervise a Bible study, but I knew God was at work; I believed he would confirm her in her salvation and open up her understanding of the Word. By that time, she was showing signs of mild dementia. I don't know how much she retained, but she was feeding her spirit just the same.

For thirteen years I drove one-hundred miles every two weeks to take her shopping, pay her bills, and take her for a ride. It got to the point where she became a danger to herself. One day I could smell gas as I opened the front door, and Mom was standing in the kitchen preparing to strike a match. "Don't light it," I yelled. Afterward I thanked God for his amazing timing and for keeping her safe.

Another time, she held the newspaper over a burner and it caught fire. The smoke alarm screamed, but she didn't know what it was. The next-door neighbor, a medical doctor, came over to help. Fortunately, Mom recognized her and opened the door; otherwise the whole house could have gone up in flames. The doctor saved her life.

It was obvious she needed a conservator, and since my sister lived in Chicago, the job fell to me. It was not difficult to obtain. Several people attested to the need. It was granted none too soon.

Mom's cataracts had reached the point she could barely see. But she refused to have surgery, saying she'd rather go blind. One of the first things I did as her conservator was to arrange for her to have them removed, one at a time. She was instructed to keep her one eye closed the rest of the day. I was amused at the fact she did remember that!

When Mary came for a visit, she found someone at Mom's church who had experience with in-home care and was looking for a job. We hired her on the spot, hoping to keep Mom at home the rest of her life. They hit it off; Mom was able to stay there eight more years until the attendant began slacking off, ignoring Mom's hacking cough without giving her anything to ease the discomfort, leaving early so she could see a favorite TV show, etc.

When Corinne, Mom's niece, retired, I asked her to be co-conservator with me. She lived much closer to Mom, and

I was still working. She agreed to help, and relieved me of some errands and the responsibility for arranging home repairs, among other things. Eventually, she found an assisted living facility near her home, and we agreed to move Mom there.

We devised a plan. I would take Mom out to eat and for a ride. Corinne would stay at the house while the movers loaded the van. Mary would go to the living facility, receive the furniture, and direct the movers where to place it so it looked familiar to Mom. And it did. Mom's response when we arrived was, "This looks like home."

She lived there seven years until she developed a physical condition they couldn't accommodate. From there she went to a care home where she passed away at one-hundred years of age just after the year turned 2000. Mom was born in 1899 and lived in three centuries. She was an extraordinary woman.

Even after she went home to be with the Lord she was testing us. After Dad passed away, Mom made a new will, dividing Dad's hard-earned assets among six heirs: Mary and me and four of Mom's nieces and nephews. I'm so glad Dad never knew that. What he had intended only for us was distributed among so many. Presented with a final chance to be mad at her, though, I found myself forgiving her. What once had been such a struggle had become an automatic response.

Now if unpleasant memories come to mind, they don't bother me; instead, I picture Mom as she is now—happy to be reunited with her son, Billy, and her family, pain-free and provided for, totally loved and accepted in Christ, knowing now what a good God he really is. God does the work of salvation; but in this case, he had to do a work in me first.

Ellen Cardwell was raised in San Francisco and lived most of her adult life in the East Bay. The majority of those years were spent raising two children and helping her husband with his business. On becoming empty nesters, Don and Ellen moved to a pretty little town on the western slope of the Sierra Nevadas.

After becoming a widow and seeking God's direction for the future, Ellen attended a Christian Writer's Conference at Mount Hermon. There she heard Ethel Herr state our goal is to glorify God, not to be published. That remains her motivation as she continues learning the craft.

As Ellen began putting into words what God had put in her heart, she found a way to reach others beyond her immediate circle of influence. For instance, the devotionals written for *The Upper Room* are translated into thirty-nine languages and read by two million people worldwide. Now Ellen is expanding her range into writing longer pieces that allow for further development of ideas. Visit her on the web at: www.ellencardwell.com.

8
WALKING MY MOTHER HOME
by Ardis A. Nelson

"I can do all this through him who gives me strength."
-Philippians 4:13

On a sunny Seattle day in July 2009 my miniature schnauzer, Zoe, reminded me it was time for her walk. We trudged up the hill toward the neighborhood park, Zoe pulling me all the way. As we reached the park, my cell phone rang. The caller ID said it was my younger brother, Glen[1]. He lived outside of St. Louis, Missouri, about two miles from the nursing home where our mother resided. She had been placed in a nursing home seven years earlier due to her mental disorders and inability to care for herself.

My heart jumped in my chest. He rarely called to just chat. It was usually about a change in Mother's health condition. I answered the phone, mentally preparing for the worst.

"Hi, Glen."

"Ardis," he said through tears. "It's Mom. We're at the hospital. She can hardly talk and her right side is paralyzed."

I stopped dead in my tracks, shocked by Glen's news, but Zoe kept pulling. This was not going to be a simple "walk and talk" cell-phone conversation. I pulled Zoe back alongside me and tried to take in everything Glen said.

"What?" I asked, not really prepared for this after all.

---

1. Some names have been changed to protect the privacy of individuals.

"The doctor is here and needs our permission to treat Mom. They want to put her on blood thinners, but there are risks involved."

"What kind of risks?"

"She could die if we treat her—or if we don't."

"I don't understand," I sobbed, pacing around the vacant playground area of the park. "Let me talk to the doctor."

"This is Dr. Halder, your mother's doctor. I need permission to treat her," he said in a thick accent. "She needs to be put on a blood thinner to dissolve any potential blood clots. But this may cause internal bleeding on the brain."

I questioned him about the prognosis and ramifications. Evidently Mom had a stroke, but the doctor wouldn't confirm that. His answers were short; he seemed impatient with my questions. We were trying to make a life-or-death decision and needed more information. The prognosis was grave; it seemed like a no-win situation. Finally, Glen and I talked more and agreed on the recommended course of treatment.

I was not close to my mother. She had suffered a nervous breakdown when I was six years old. My older brother, John, was ten at the time, and Glen was a month-old baby.

I was too young to remember, but was told that one day she just "snapped." All indications are that, up to that point in time, she was a sane woman.

One Sunday morning in January 1966, Mom dressed Glen in a christening gown for his baptism at the Catholic church. Unfortunately, she didn't remember that he had already been baptised the week before. Mom became delusional and by the next day, she was admitted to a psychiatric hospital for treatment.

During one of these first stays in the mental hospital Mom was given shock treatment, and she was never the same after that. It wiped out many of her memories and affected her ability to emotionally bond with others. Of course, I didn't realize these things until much later in life.

When I was growing up, nothing about my mother seemed out of the ordinary to me. She maintained the household and prepared the family meals. I don't remember her being a happy person, but now realize she was medicated most of the time. I knew that she regularly attended a psychiatrist, though I didn't fully understand why. It was never discussed. Except for her depression, she seemed normal. My father never criticized her. Then out of the blue, three years after Mom's nervous breakdown, my parents divorced. Dad sent Mom and us kids back to the St. Louis area to be near Mom's family.

Our new family environment was chaotic and dysfunctional. Mom remarried, but our stepfather was an alcoholic. Shortly after that, John was sent to live with Dad in Oregon. When I went away to college, Glen was left to fend for himself and care for Mom, where he has remained throughout his life.

After I left home, Mom, diagnosed with schizophrenia, was in and out of mental hospitals. For my own sense of sanity, I kept her at a distance from me and my family. On the few occasions I tried to connect with her, I didn't trust what she told me. I never knew what mood she'd be in, whether she'd be coherent or lost in her own little world. Later when I did try to reach out to her, she refused my calls. So I pretty much wrote off my mother. It was just too painful to be her daughter. All I could "see" was that she was crazy.

Writing my mother off started many years ago, mostly because it was too emotionally agonizing to see her in such a mental state, but also because of the fears I had that I would someday be like her. Growing up, I internalized the subtle messages that my emotions were not something I should share and in fact, that if I did, there must be something wrong with me—like my mother. Fearful of becoming crazy, I learned to shut down my emotions and not share them with anyone.

After I married, my mother started calling me in the middle of the night. She'd say bizarre, alarming things, demanding money or yelling at me. She also sent me letters, in which she would profess her love for my father, who by then was remarried. Sometimes she would include Catholic prayer cards, which at the time I didn't welcome. The letters stopped not long after she went into the nursing home.

As I witnessed her deterioration with the eyes of an adult, I began to question my own mental health. I was depressed much of the time and didn't have much joy in my life. As I continued to stuff my emotions, lurking in the back of my mind was the subconscious message that one day I could "snap." On the occasions when my emotions got to be too much for me, I would hide in my room and just let the tears flow. I was afraid to seek medical help or take drugs. I was afraid of being locked up like my mother.

Finally, when Mother's mental health deteriorated to the point that she refused medical care, Glen became her surrogate decision maker for health matters. He would call me for advice, and we'd try to logically and prayerfully decide what to do next. Those calls were rare, though.

This call marked the beginning of a new era for me and my mother. I said good-bye to Glen and hurried with Zoe back to the house. Then I called Aunt Mary, Mom's only living sibling who lived ten miles away from her. They hadn't seen each other for a few years. Mary, who was dealing with her own difficult life situation as the caretaker for her adult son, Mark, rarely left their home and didn't drive.

"Aunt Mary, this is Ardis."

"Oh, Ardis, how nice to hear from you!"

"I hate to tell you this, but I have bad news. Mom is in the hospital, and it doesn't look good. They think it's a stroke."

"Oh no, Ardis. That is so sad."

"Look, Aunt Mary, they don't know if she is going to make it through this. So I suggest, if you want to see your sister alive again, try to go to the hospital as soon as possible." It was hard to keep calm. I urged Mary to go, since I couldn't.

Although Mary seemed to hesitate, she did visit her sister the next day. The report I got back from her was very optimistic. She said my mother looked good, was in strong spirits considering her condition, and could even say Mark's name. Mary said she had prayed over her sister.

This was all welcome news. Each day I would call the hospital to get a report of Mom's condition. They weren't committing to a prognosis or estimating the length of her hospital stay. They were taking it a day at a time. The test results revealed that she had had a massive stroke and a small heart attack. After several days, she returned to the nursing home where they gave her occupational and physical therapy.

It seemed, then, that she was out of the woods. My father had recovered from a stroke a few years prior, so I had hope that she would fully recover also. My life returned to normal—caring for my husband and two teenage sons: Our older son, Evan, was starting his senior year in high school and our younger, Cameron, was entering junior high. Any ideas or thoughts I had about making a trip back home to Illinois vanished. Totally immersed again in my own family life, two months later I got another phone call.

It was Glen. Mom was again in the hospital—with a minor heart attack this time. I discovered that no one had ever filed a "Do Not Resuscitate" order for her. With no DNR on file, my siblings and I were faced with making many difficult decisions on how invasive her care should be.

The last time I had seen my mother was one-and-a-half

years earlier. I was in Wisconsin to acquire a bequest from the estate of Aunt Ardis, my father's sister and my godmother. A snowstorm had cancelled my flight back to Seattle, but I had been able to reroute my flight through St. Louis. Glen had picked me up at the airport and took me to the nursing home for a short visit. Mother was not expecting me.

"You're not Ardis," she said. "You're too fat to be Ardis."

"Mom, of course, it's me. I'm Ardis, your daughter."

But she insisted I was not!

"I'll prove it to you, Mom." I pulled out my driver's license.

She looked at the license, and she didn't look very happy with the idea of me being her daughter. However, she was clearly not coherent, making little sense in conversation. Finally, I said my good-byes but broke down in tears as I left the building. I fully expected that the next call I would get about my mother would be of her death. And that was all right with me.

But God, it seemed, had other ideas.

Over the past ten years, I had been seeking God's will in my life. I grew up Catholic but turned away from the church in my youth. As a young adult, I rededicated my life to Christ. When I went away to college, I joined the Christian fellowship on campus, eager to study the Bible. When I got married, though, I again turned away from the faith.

After having children, I went to a Protestant church and started attending Bible studies, retreats, and spiritual growth classes. I attended Celebrate Recovery, Christian 12-Step meetings that helped me to share my vulnerability and face my brokenness. It was in these meetings that I was able to see I was not alone and that sharing my emotions was a healthy thing to do. Jesus became real to me, but I still had a deep hole inside. It was hard for me to look at the pain left in my heart from the lack of a mother's love.

As I approached menopause, I experienced new dimensions of that loss, not having a mother whom I could query life's challenges or from whom I could seek guidance.

Then the Lord placed a heavy burden on my heart to go back to Illinois to be with my mother. It was not a decision that I took lightly or eagerly embraced. But in my Christian walk, as the Holy Spirit had led me through challenging situations, God had always comforted and strengthened me through them. He kept building my faith in that way. Now it was time for me to take this step of obedience, leaving the results, and everything to do with my relationship with my mother, up to God. Taking this trip back home would strain our finances. It would create logistic problems with the kids' routines. As I prepared for the trip, though, I kept clinging to my life verse: "Trust in the LORD with all your heart and lean not on your own understanding; in all your ways submit to him, and he will direct your paths" (Proverbs 3:5-6).

Even though I knew that God called me to go to my mother, the challenge became when and how to fit it into my schedule. My fiftieth birthday was coming in the next few weeks, with a party planned. And I had volunteered to help at a New Life Ministries weekend. How would this trip fit in? I ended up buying airline tickets to leave immediately following my ministry obligation and returned four days later. This would get me back home in time for my birthday party with a few days to spare. It was a relief to have the trip all planned.

Six days before my scheduled flight to Illinois, another call came from the nursing home. Karen, the director of nursing, said Mom was unresponsive, not eating, and in grave condition. I gave them permission to rush her to the hospital. Since the DNR was not yet signed, Glen and I jumped into action to get his virtual signature via fax on the legal documents. On pins and needles all day, I cried and prayed, talked with staff at the ER, and sent out e-mail prayer requests. I also checked on airfares to change my flight and leave right away. I didn't think she would make it. Had God really told me to go and be with her?

But Mother pulled through this medical emergency also. The doctors recommended a minor procedure to insert a feeding tube into her stomach—for precautionary purposes, just in case she stopped eating again. It was intended to supplement her meals. We gave our permission, not realizing this was one of the heroic, life-saving measures we had intended to avoid. I just thanked God for giving me a second chance to see her.

The next few days passed slowly. As I served at the local New Life Ministries weekend event, my heart was in Illinois with my mother. The message of the event was, "Living life without regrets." This was just what I needed to hear, giving me courage to get on that plane the next day. And what a blessing to be supported in prayer by the ministry staff.

Still, when my friend Janet took me to the airport the next morning, I broke down in tears. Everything hit me. This trip would be difficult physically and emotionally; I dreaded it. I couldn't bear the thought of seeing my mother in that state. I was scared, not knowing what to expect.

I landed in St. Louis early evening, exhausted, sore, and hungry. Glen and his wife, Betty, met me at the hotel about a mile from the nursing home. Visiting Mom was the first thing on the agenda; dinner would have to wait. They had moved Mom to the very back of the building, at the end of a long hallway. As the three of us walked to her room, Betty held my hand and prayed with me.

"Lord, help me get through this," I prayed. "Help me to be a loving daughter, and give me strength."

As we walked down the hallways, the sights, sounds, and smells of the nursing home accosted my senses: sterile yet stale. Residents with mobility were free to wander outside their rooms, and there was a continual sound of slippered feet scuffling across the floor.

Stopping at the door to my mother's room. I took in a deep breath, said another quick prayer, forced a smile, and walked into the room.

Mother was expecting us this time. The room contained three beds, but only two were in use. Her bed was farthest from the door, near the window. Her roommate was not in the room when we arrived. Mom was lying in her bed, her back propped up at a 45-degree angle. She peered into space. Glen approached the bed first.

"Momma, there's someone here to see you." Glen paused and waited, until she acknowledged him with her eyes. "It's Ardis," he continued. "Ardis is here from Seattle." He motioned his head toward me as I walked up to her bed.

I smiled and gently took her right hand. Her arthritis and paralysis were so severe, that the nurses had wrapped her fingers around a tiny pillow designed to keep her hand from closing completely shut. She nodded her head repeatedly and grinned. She looked intently into my eyes. My heart melted as I fought back tears.

"Momma, it's Ardis. I'm here for you. I'm so sorry I wasn't here sooner. I love you." My words ran together as I bent over to kiss her forehead.

Externally she did not look like my mother. In my mind my mother was still an auburn-haired beauty. The seventy-eight-year-old woman before me looked much older. She still had a beautiful head of long hair, now silver; though she had pulled a lot of it out after the stroke.

She was frail. The right side of her body was limp and her speech limited. Most of her communication was done by nodding for "yes" and shaking her head for "no." At times those gestures were confusing. But when the answer to a request was "no," that word seemed to have no problem coming out, in much the same way a toddler makes her needs emphatically known.

She managed to say my name, "Ardis Ann," and "love you." This was music to my ears. And when she couldn't speak or utter those words, she would wink at me.

The next three days flew by. I met with the social worker, Melanie, nursing director, Karen, and the occupational therapist. I fed Mom, monitored her food intake, and helped her adjust to her new level of health care. It was painful to see her so helpless. The nurse's aides used a hydraulic lift fitted with a hammock to put her in the geri-chair, a recliner on wheels. Twice a day they wheeled her to the dining area. Being around others at mealtime was supposed to stimulate her to want to eat.

I had envisioned reading Bible verses and sharing my faith with her. I expected that there would be "down time" when I could read and relax awhile with her. It didn't work out that way. It was not, as I had expected it to be, like a Hollywood movie with me doting on her.

I would generally be with her for lunch and dinner. After feeding her dinner, I would drag myself back to the hotel room, have a late dinner, relax in the hot tub, call my husband and friends back home asking for prayer support, then crash. And do it all over again the next day.

When the day came to fly back home, I felt God saying it wasn't time to leave yet. My staying meant canceling my fiftieth birthday party and spending my birthday away from family and friends. The more I prayed about it, though, the more I had peace about that decision.

My brother John made the decision easier for me by paying the extra costs for the trip. The extra days also allowed me the opportunity to handle hospice arrangements, meet with the chaplain, and since Mom was Catholic, have a priest perform an anointing of the sick for her. John was in the loop on all of Mom's medical decisions, but didn't originally feel the need to visit. I was relieved when he and his wife, Carol, agreed to return with me for another trip in December.

My birthday was a bittersweet day. It was a day of giving and receiving. I fed my mother and massaged her feet, organized her personal belongings, had a digital photo album made, and bought her a few small gifts, including a rosary that she clutched in her left hand. I told her she brought me into the world and cared for me as a baby fifty years ago; and now I was doing these things for her. I took my first communion cross that I received from my godmother, Aunt Ardis, off my neck and put it on Mom's. I didn't want to part with that cross, but I felt she needed it more than I did.

"Mom, I'm giving this cross to you now. It's my promise to return to see you."

She smiled and winked at me.

"I'll be back in a few weeks with John. So don't go anywhere, Mom. I'll be back."

She acknowledged me again with a wink and a nod.

I fought tears and prayed all the way to the car. "Lord, please keep her alive to have one last reunion with all three of her children. Lord, I know you wanted me here for a reason and I pray that you will bless my mother and our family with wholeness and restoration, and let Mom go in peace."

The next three weeks flew by with Thanksgiving and Christmas preparations. Soon I was flying back to Illinois. My flight into St. Louis arrived a few hours before John and his wife, Carol, arrived from Portland, Oregon. I waited for them, and since I had a miserable trip—losing my contacts while passing through security, my luggage not making the connecting flight—I was grateful to share the ride from the airport with John and Carol.

One of the first things I noticed when we saw Mom was that the cross pendant I left on her neck the previous visit was gone. It wasn't a total surprise to me; I had learned years ago to never give my mother expensive gifts. They would always end up lost or stolen. This time I wasn't bothered by the loss, though. I knew it was the giving of the gift that was important. That was one of many shifts I noticed God doing in my heart.

We had only two days with Mom. She was very happy to see all of us—John, Glen, and me. John tried to get her to communicate by writing the alphabet on a sheet of paper and getting her to spell out words. But it was a fruitless effort. Although John didn't have a need for closure with Mom, he did communicate later that he was thankful we had this experience together.

We also met with her health-care providers and decided to not send her to the hospital anymore—no more heroic measures. We just wanted her to be comfortable. We also made the arrangements for her funeral services. It brought more relief to have these decisions handled.

When the time came to say our final good-byes, God had it perfectly scripted. John did most of the talking, which was a welcome change for me.

On my first trip home to see her, she had told me she wasn't ready to see Jesus. But when we asked her this time she said, "Yes." That was a wonderful surprise.

I had expected a heart-wrenching, tearful good-bye between us, but that didn't happen. I left sad but joyous and peaceful about having gotten some closure. I believed she was at peace with her life and where she was going to spend eternity.

After this trip, I was on a spiritual high. There was much healing and restoration between my brothers and me. There was also bonding with both of my sisters-in-law. Thinking that Mom's death would come soon, my life returned to the normal routine of busyness and caretaking for my family. Evan was in the peak of the college-selection process. I wanted to visit my mother again, but any travel plans were put on hold until we knew which colleges to visit in the spring.

During this time, I routinely called to check in on my mother and ask the staff to communicate my love to her.

Days turned into weeks, and weeks turned into months. Living with uncertainties—of Mom's final days and of my son's future—caused me to slide into a depression. Evan eventually decided to attend a university in-state. We were glad that he wasn't going to be far from home.

In April 2010, I got another emergency call from the nursing home. They reported that Mother had bruising on her right leg and they needed permission to send her to the hospital for X-rays. The nurse explained that they had launched an investigation into the matter, which is routine procedure whenever patient bruising occurred. A feeling of helplessness came over me. I was 2,000 miles away.

Again I felt God telling me that I needed to go back home. Since Evan was going to be attending college in-state, and didn't need travel funds, I was able to purchase airline tickets for a short trip to be with Mom over Mother's Day.

Nothing prepared me, though, to deal with the deterioration in my mother's health condition. She was now totally immobile, with her leg in a splint. Even with the hydraulic lift, it was extremely difficult to move her to the geri-chair.

There were multiple possibilities for the cause of the bruising, and they were all medically related, with no trauma involved. She had severe osteoarthritis. They suspected she had multiple myeloma, a form of cancer that eats away at the bones and makes them frail. This meant that her leg wasn't the only extremity of concern. Testing for this disease was pretty invasive and there was no treatment for it; so we declined. The staff was very good at monitoring her pain and medicating her as necessary. I hated to see her have to endure what seemed like senseless suffering in her passing.

Mom's speech was virtually gone. She could no longer say my name. She could still manage to occasionally say "no" and could audibly moan and groan—not happy sounds. Her solid food intake was non-existent except for occasional "pleasure" foods, as the nursing-home staff called them. Gone were the special bonding times when I could feed her. She received her nourishment from the feeding tube.

The one bit of joy I received on this trip was in bringing Aunt Mary to visit her. It was a tearful visit. We prayed together over Mom. I took pictures as I did on the other visits and bought my mother a bracelet and another rosary.

When I left, there was no spiritual high. I was thankful to have had this extra time with Mom. I had served her and loved her as best I could. I felt I had given her all I could give. But God gave me the strength to say good-bye again.

Over the next few months, my life turned back to normal as we focused on Evan's final days in high school. He was a gifted classical pianist and performed at the baccalaureate service. He also had a graduation party at the house.

In the midst of all this end-of-high-school activity we were asked to open our home to an exchange student for one month during the summer. My husband and I had done this many years ago, before we had kids, and had wanted to do it again. We liked the idea of a short-term exchange program as a way to introduce our kids to other cultures, so we agreed to participate in the program.

I didn't know what to expect, adding a guest to our home and family. My heart was still back in Illinois with my mother, but there was nothing I could do except pray and wait for God's timing. One week before the arrival of Pedro, our host son from Spain, I prayed that God would help me to model Christianity, to "go with the flow," and to embrace my role as a mom to three teenage young men.

Pedro was an engaging young man with an eagerness to learn about American culture and history. He was very social and entertaining, with a warmth and sense of humor that kept us all in stitches. He was also a practicing Catholic. Pedro's arrival and smooth integration into our family was just what I needed to forget my troubles and see life from a different perspective—one with sightseeing and lots of laughs. It was medicine to my soul.

The month that Pedro stayed with us flew by quickly. Almost daily we explored Washington state together, and Pedro became like family to us. I even started to communicate by e-mail with his mother, Rosa, during that time. He gave me much joy in the midst of my pain over my mother's long passing. After Pedro left, there seemed to be a hole left in my heart. What I didn't know then was how God had ordained this relationship to foster the final healing I needed concerning my mother.

I had led support and women's groups at my church and participated in the women's ministry in the past. As I dealt with my mother's medical condition and Evan's senior year in high school, I had taken a break from serving in ministry. I spent time in prayer after completing a summer Bible study, and was seeking God's will for where I was to serve in ministry for this next season of my life. That is when I sensed the Lord telling me to "invest in people."

When Pedro returned to his home in Madrid, we continued our relationship via e-mail and Skype calls. Pedro shared the sad news that his grandmother, Carmen, Rosa's mother, had just been diagnosed with a cancerous brain tumor. Her prognosis was grim, and she was expected to live only a few more months. My heart ached for them.

I felt this was an opportunity to "invest in people," so I started to communicate more with Rosa. Neither one of us spoke the other's native language, but we were able to use an online translator. We had just started to do that when I got the news about Pedro's grandmother. As sad as it was, I felt God had put our families together so Rosa and I could minister to each other in the passing of our mothers. Although we were continents apart and didn't speak the same language, and I was Protestant and she was Catholic, we did worship the same God. We e-mailed back and forth our prayers and encouragement to each other. Her words touched my heart. It gave me hope to know that I was not in this alone.

As my fifty-first birthday and the holidays approached, I couldn't help but think about my trips back home to see my mother the year before. I had been so sure that Mom would not survive another year.

Then on January 12, 2011, I got a call from the nursing home requesting to send my mother to the hospital for a simple routine procedure to replace her feeding tube. As I prayed about this, it came to my mind to ask Mom what *she* wanted. So we made arrangements for the people who knew her best to meet with her at the hospital to help decipher her answer. Glen and Betty were there, along with nurse Kendra and Father Leonard from the hospice organization.

It was a difficult conversation; Mom couldn't talk. It was also emotionally painful, with life-and-death consequences. They explained to her in as simple terms as they could that the feeding tube needed to be replaced. They told her that the tube was her main source for nourishment. They asked her if she wanted it replaced. They asked her if she was ready to meet Jesus. All of her nodding and "no" responses seemed to consistently indicate her desire to proceed with the surgery.

While they were meeting with my mother at the hospital, I was home, praying, pleading with God for a clear answer. I asked him to give me peace about her decision, whatever it was. I knew it was either going to be the beginning of the end for us or a continuation of waiting for God to take her home. When Glen called to tell me what happened, I was surprised and somewhat confused. I had thought God was saying it was her time to go.

On the heels of this medical situation, we got the news that Pedro's grandmother had died. In a short e-mail, Pedro told us the sad news. He said we were part of his family for "the good *and* bad things." I immediately replied with e-mails to Rosa and Pedro expressing my heartache for their loss and prayers for their family.

Since I grew up Catholic, I knew it was customary to have a Mass said when a person dies. So I made arrangements at the local parish in town to have a Mass said for Carmen. While there, I requested a Mass for my mother's illness also. The next available date for this type of Mass just happened to fall on the same date as Carmen's funeral in Spain. With the nine-hour time difference between our locations, my mother's Mass ended at the same time Carmen's funeral began in Spain. This was one of many circumstances between our families that felt God-anointed.

While still in the Roman Catholic church, and during Carmen's funeral Mass in Spain, I lit a candle and knelt to pray. During this time of solitude and sanctity, I fervently prayed for both mothers. It was an amazing spiritual experience that allowed me to surrender the timing of my mother's passing, and to let go of any expectations of when I would see her again. I also sensed God telling me to continue to write to my mother. I left the church with complete peace, trusting God with the outcome.

Less than two weeks later, I was on my way to my friend Linda's house, when I received a message on my cell phone from the nursing home.

"Ardis, this is Wendy at Life Giving Health Care. I am calling to let you know that your mother's health is declining.

You can call us back and ask to speak to Donna."

My heart raced. Ever since I had started down this medical road with my mother, I had dreaded a call that would tell me she had passed away or a call like this one that said there were visible signs of her decline. When I called back, the nurse defined "decline" more specifically for me.

"Ardis, your mother is not going to make it through the night."

"But I live in Seattle! I can't get there until tomorrow!" On a previous conversation with Karen, the nursing director had explained that when the body shuts down, there are visible signs, and the death process could take a few days. That is what I expected. But now Mom had had another stroke, and her body was rapidly shutting down.

"I'm sorry, Ardis, but your mother is in respiratory distress. Her body is in the dying process. She is not going to make it through the night." She further explained that my mother had no circulation, cold feet and arms, a temperature of 100.3, was gasping for air, and turning blue.

I called and talked with my brother Glen, who had just arrived at the nursing home, along with his wife, Betty. They were with Mom. Through tears he tried to update me on what was going on there. She was truly close to passing on.

As this reality sank in, I prayed silently to help me calm down and focus on what my mother and brother needed at the moment. I asked Glen to put his cell phone on the speaker setting, so I could talk to Mom and pray for her.

My friend Linda helped me book the next possible flight to St. Louis. Unfortunately that wasn't until 5:15 the next morning, which would get me to St. Louis at two o'clock in the afternoon.

There was nothing else I could do for my mother. I hurriedly packed. I was still awake when Glen called just after 1:00 a.m. my time to tell me that our mother had died. I broke down in tears. My mother was dead.

I sent an e-mail to Pedro:

> *Pedro, I am writing to you because it is too hard for me right now to use the translator, etc., to write your mother. I am packing for my flight to St. Louis. My mother passed away about 45 minutes ago. I am numb. I must finish well for my mother and do what needs to be done for her. She is now at peace, along with your grandmother. How beautiful is that? It makes me smile to think about that. Please tell your mother this news for me. Love, Ardis*

I followed that e-mail with one to my friends asking for prayer for my trip and posted the same on Facebook.

The next several days in Illinois were a whirlwind of activities. Over the past eighteen months it seemed God had been preparing me to do some bold things in obedience to him. Each time I would take one of those steps, I would doubt what I was doing and have fear about completing the task. But as I chose to lean on God, he would comfort and uphold me through each difficulty. Each day on this final trip back home held special significance in my healing process.

DAY 1

I wanted to see my mother's body before the cremation. We were allowed only one viewing. I felt God had laid it on my heart to wash her feet. So I asked the funeral director and invited Glen and Betty to participate in the "ceremony."

On my first visit to see my mother back in November 2009, I had massaged her feet. It was a small way to serve her and show love to her. It was similar to how Jesus cleaned the feet of the disciples. I had my feet washed at a women's retreat a few years prior and felt so humbled by the experience. I wanted to do this one last act of humility and honor for my mother. The funeral home was very gracious in grant-

ing my request. The final viewing and ceremony were scheduled for the next day.

DAY 2

At the nursing home we met with Melanie, Mom's social
worker, and with Father Leonard to plan her memorial service. The recent passing of Rosa's mother had acquainted me
with what to expect in burying my mother according to her
Catholic faith.

My next step of obedience was offering to do my mother's eulogy at the nursing home memorial service in two days.

Karen, the nursing director, told me about the details of
my mother's death. She said Mother's countenance or presence changed to a more peaceful state about two weeks prior
to her death. That was the exact time I had prayed for her
in the Catholic church! With tears, I told Karen about the
significance of what she had just told me. As a practicing
Protestant I had submitted myself to the ways of a practicing
Catholic by having a Mass said, lighting a candle, and praying there for my mother. Then, within a few weeks, Rosa's
mother and my mother were united in heaven.

Later that day we went to the funeral home for the final
viewing of Mom's body. We were met there by Father Leonard
for final words before the cremation. The viewing and foot
washing was a beautiful time of reflection, of honoring and
mourning our mother. God held me up and comforted me.

DAY 3

I spent the day in my hotel room alone, creating a program
for the memorial service and writing the eulogy. God showed
up throughout the day, giving me glimpses of how he created
me like my mother in so many ways. The eulogy gave me a
way to share about the legacy my mother left me.

I reflected on the beauty of my mother, whereas before I

had only seen her through the lens of her craziness, her mental illness. God showed me that I was made in my mother's likeness: her love of photography, music, and dance; her flair for style and love of life; and her emotional sensitivity.

Above all else, my mother left me a legacy of faith as she instilled a love for Jesus in me. One of the ways she did this was through her letters, which were filled with scripture or a prayer. She had been praying for me for years, as witnessed through those letters. Unfortunately I didn't recognize her heart and her faith in them. Her letters were much like the ones I had been writing lately to Rosa and Pedro, but I didn't see the connection until that day as I wrote her eulogy.

DAY 4

"I can do all this through him who gives me strength" (Philippians 4:13). That verse kept going through my mind and prayers as I mustered up the courage and strength to speak at my mother's first memorial service, one of the most difficult things I had ever done. The room was filled with nursing-home staff and residents who had known Mom in recent years much better than I had. I opened my heart to them and shared with them the beauty that God had shown me in my mother. I tried to paint a picture of a different woman, not the hysterical, crazy woman they saw, but the beautiful woman that she was on the inside before her illness captured her and stole her mind.

After the service, I had the opportunity to give my testimony at a local Celebrate Recovery meeting. I regularly attended these meetings where I lived and had given my testimony several times. Glen and his wife joined me at the meeting. It was painful to share my testimony, with these new revelations, so soon. As a facilitator of support groups, though, I knew the importance of modeling vulnerability and brokenness to provide hope and encouragement for others.

So I took this step. All I can do is take one day at a time and trust God each step of the way.

DAY 5

My last day in Illinois was reserved for a small memorial service at the funeral home and the gravesite burial ceremony. This time Aunt Mary and her family were present at the service. Reading the eulogy the second time around wasn't much easier. It was during this service, though, that I was able to publicly thank my aunt for her intercessory prayer at my mother's hospital bedside immediately following the first stroke. Her prayer was the life-giving measure that allowed me to see my mother alive again and set in motion the events that followed. It gave me the second chance to make things right with my mother.

At the gravesite, we prayed as a family over Mom's remains and covered them with dirt in her final resting place.

"Thank you, Mom, for the gift you gave me. May you rest in peace," I prayed silently. Then I added, "Thank you, Lord, for your healing."

As the days passed I continued to embrace the transformation that God had done in me. I was embracing the parts of my mother that were in me. My mother was gone. She was resting in peace, as was Carmen, Rosa's mother. I felt freer. I felt alive. I felt my mother's presence with me and I felt her joy. It was all because of the blessing of God's miraculous healing.

The part that the Catholic church played in this was particularly significant to me as well. While my mother had remained a practicing Catholic all her life, I never went through the rite of confirmation and eventually chose a different path of faith in the Protestant church. In the past I had been critical of the Roman Catholic Church, but my openness to healing led to acceptance of the differences between these faiths. After years of misunderstanding, it was very gratifying to be able to get in touch with my Catholic roots and experience God there in a reverent way. This connection also helped cement a bond across the distance between Rosa and me.

When God started to point me in the direction of this healing back in November 2009, I knew that I had to walk through the pain to get to the other side, to wholeness. He had shown me this in the past, and as scary as it was, I knew it was time to step up for the next layer of healing. I had to lose myself (see Matthew 16:24) so I could be and do what was needed for my mother. In the process, God gave me back a life that is richly filled with his joy and peace.

My biggest fear was eliminated as a result of this journey. I have total confidence in my ability to say that I am not crazy and that God gave me emotional sensitivity for a reason. It is the way I give back to others—through compassion and empathy. It is what I used to connect with Rosa as she grieved the loss of her mother. Her acceptance of that in me gave me the confidence to stay connected with her across 5,300 miles and beyond our language barrier, though we had never met in person.

Aside from the spiritual and emotional healing I received, there was one very special physical gift that I also received. When Pedro returned to visit that summer, Rosa gave me a sterling silver cross pendant. Neither she nor Pedro knew that I had given my cross to my mother on my fiftieth birthday. It seemed to me that God beautifully orchestrated the receipt of a new cross that would have significance to me. This new cross was a reminder of Rosa's and my love for each other, our love for our mothers, and our love for God.

What I learned through this healing journey is that sometimes we really don't need to know the answers to why God allows the trials and tribulations in our lives. Sometimes we just need to take him at his word and trust that he will make all things right if we surrender to his will. God's timing really is perfect. We need to step out in faith and do that next bold act of obedience that he is calling us to do.

Ardis A. Nelson is a wife of twenty-nine years and a mother of two teenage young men. She has what she considers "extended family" in Spain, including a young man who she affectionately considers her son, and his mother.

Residing with her family and a miniature schnauzer named Zoe, in the suburbs of Seattle, Washington, Ardis's hobbies and spare time are devoted to photography, scrapbooking, reading, and memoir writing.

Her ministry passion is facilitating spiritual growth and support groups for women. She has been active in organizing women's retreats and events, speaking at women's functions and sharing her testimony at recovery group meetings. Her writing includes e-devotionals for her church and regularly blogging at www.ardisanelson.com/makingmebold/. She can be contacted at info@ardisanelson.com.

9
WHITE KNUCKLES
by Loritta Slayton

"Love must be sincere ... cling to what is good."
-Romans 12:9

Ka-plunk! The freezer-burned leftovers landed inside the big black garbage bag beside me. My "Raid on Entebbe," as my husband Michael called it, was underway. In the historic Raid on Entebbe, the Israelis used stealth to free their citizens who were held hostage. I too, was using stealth; this was all happening while my mom was away. I planned it that way in order to avoid as much conflict as possible. I hated facing conflict with my mother.

A considerable amount of the food in my mom's refrigerator and freezer was in varied stages of spoilage or freezer burn. Besides the food, there was an excess supply of take-home boxes and other things that she relentlessly saved! There were sanitation requirements necessary for her to remain as a resident in this place. I was here to accomplish the task.

I had about an hour or so before she would arrive home. I moved quickly, filling a couple of trash bags easily. I intended to get them to the Dumpster before her return, to prevent her from attempting to retrieve what was being thrown out. As the time for her return drew near, I sent my husband out for guard duty. He was to let me know when she arrived in the parking lot, allowing me time to clear the trash from the kitchen.

194

Mom shared an apartment with my mother-in-law, Pat, at the independent living senior facility in town. Pat was now there reminding me, "Your mom is going to be mad!"

"I don't care! This has to be done! She can't keep all this stuff!"

My heartbeat quickened as I raced to finish before Michael would return to inform me of my mom's imminent return. I not only felt anxious, but irritated. I didn't like this job. I didn't like having to take my time and energy to do what she should already have the sense and ability to do herself! I'd been cleaning up after my mom since I was a kid. Her unreasonableness infuriated me. Suddenly, the door opened and there stood—Mom! I saw the dreaded look of disapproval. She began telling me how she didn't like what I was doing. I felt flushed and angry. Where was Michael, anyway? How had Mom slipped past his watchful eye? What had gone wrong?

"Mom, you can't keep all this junk! You have to get rid of it. The facility doesn't want this kind of mess in your refrigerator."

It was too late! The conflict was on! She was upset and agitated, and I was getting angrier by the moment! Why didn't she appreciate all the hard work I did for her? I had taken my time and my energy for months to clear out her previous house from nearly fifty-eight years of stuff she had refused and neglected to take care of! Now she was here, with the same habits, hoarding all this waste again. She couldn't even admit it was junk. Why was she so difficult? I was fuming mad, livid in my self-righteousness.

"Mom, I love you," I said tersely, "but I am very angry right now. I'm going home. We'll talk more later."

With that, Michael and I walked out the door (with the trash). We discarded it in the Dumpster and then headed home. The emotions continued to churn and boil within me into the afternoon. Finally, I was convicted of my need to deal with this anger. Knowing from past experience that journaling would help, I picked up my journal and sat down on the couch to start defusing this nebulous mass of emotions. Taking my pen, I began to write. The emotions rolled out in a gush of words. I let it rip! At last I summarized my thoughts. "God," I seethed, "it's like she has a death grip on her d----- stuff!!!"

I paused; and in the pause I heard God's response in my heart and mind. "Yes, and you have a death grip on your emotions."

I was stunned. I pondered his words. It was as though God had shot an arrow from his quiver of truth and struck the bull's-eye of my heart! As the conviction penetrated my heart, a sudden calmness came over me. "Lord," I said, "you are right. I give you permission to start loosening my fingers from this white-knuckled grip."

> "Our iniquities, our secret heart *and* its sins [which we would so like to conceal even from ourselves], You have set in the [revealing] light of Your countenance" (Psalm 90:8, AMPLIFIED).

Reflecting back, I remember the 1960s when my family took time for daily devotions and prayer. As we sat on the matching green love seats, the cushions trimmed with fringe, I snuggled close to my mother, resting my face against the warmth of her arm. My father had struggled in school with reading, so my mother read to us from the children's Bible storybook. Listening to the easy flow of her voice reading the words, I was comforted. I loved to hear her read the familiar stories. It was one time in the day when I had a connection with her. From there, our relationship was fragmented and distant. After devotions and a quick bite to eat, we rushed off for our different agendas. My mother taught kindergarten in the public school just down the street. I was in a parochial school, and later my brother as well. My dad repaired televisions and radios.

In addition to teaching public school, my mother was talented in a number of ways. She loved plants and flowers. Our yard was enhanced by many beautiful flowers, shrubs, and trees. My parents had planted many fruit trees and nut trees, a grapevine, and a vegetable garden. All this gardening took a lot of time and attention in our large yard. My mother was skilled at flower arranging, and judged at flower shows. She was a great seamstress. She made most of my clothes, as well as her own. She loved music, teaching piano lessons to several students, including my brother and me. She sang in choral groups for church. My brother and I were given art lessons and musical instruments along with the lessons. We were given a rich heritage in numerous ways, but the development of healthy relational interactions was lacking.

The only girl in a family of seven children, my mother used to say, "I had six brothers. I was the only girl. Three brothers were older than me and three were younger. They either beat me up or beat me down!"

They lived in Harrold, Texas. My mother's family had many struggles, financially and relationally. Her mother, Bertie, was a godly woman while her father, Wade, was characterized by his anger.

Bertie had suffered many hardships in her life. She was six when her mother died and left a large family to be raised by their father. They traveled to wherever they could find work in the fields. Even so, her father had managed to keep the family together. Sometimes they lived in a tent with very little of this world's goods. But somewhere in all the darkness there was a ray of light. Someone had believed in the Bible and planted the seeds of faith. They'd taken root and borne fruit in at least some of the children. My grandmother, Bertie, was one in whose heart there was found good soil. Truth from God's Word had been established, bringing hope where hope was limited.

That hope in Christ had been handed down to my mother, and she in turn had handed it down to me. My mother, Algeritta, was the kindergarten leader for the children's ministry at our church. One morning in the kindergarten class, Mother asked us five-year-olds, "Who wants to ask Jesus to come into your heart?"

I was one who raised my hand that day. I still remember it clearly. My response was genuine and from the heart. And so I will always be grateful to my mother for the eternal investment she placed in me. A foundation had been laid, but the structure built upon it had many weaknesses.

Generational family patterns, religious legalism, and improper social thinking of the day all contributed to weak relational interactions. Conflict was stifled, diverted, or overwhelmed to the point of submission by the strongest and most aggressive. The voice of a child had little place for validation. Respect for authority was not earned as much as it was forced. Enforcement was the mode of operation rather than gentle, but firm, guidance. On both sides of my family, the grandfather was characterized by using anger to control his family and his wife. Both my father and my mother carried anger and impatience developed by their own upbringing. I'm sure they both felt that their disciplinary ways "of training us up in the way that we should go" was a far cry better than what they had received growing up; but to a large degree, it was still very hurtful, especially in the use of anger to enforce correction. It was damaging to be shouted at rather than spoken with. And so, little by little, a division was being established between parent and child. Lack of trust was prevalent. Fear was the thermometer of the relational interaction.

When I received my first kiss from a boy, I had no desire to share this with my mother. She asked me to share with her, but I declined. She expressed her disappointment in my response by saying, "I don't understand. I shared everything with my mother."

In silence, I responded within, "Yeah, I could understand you being able to share with Grandma. She's not like you." But, I said nothing.

I always felt loved and safe with Grandma. I adored her. I didn't feel the anger and impatience from her that I felt from my parents.

At fourteen, I was excited to be sent to a parochial boarding academy. I chose one that was a few hours away, realizing this would be a step of freedom from the anger and legalistic discipline I had at home. There was an academy nearby where I could have come home every day, but I didn't want that. Fortunately for me, my parents thought that the one nearby was too worldly, and the one I wanted was in good standing. You might ask the question, "How could a boarding school have more freedom than being at home?"

On a visit home from the academy one weekend, I was asked out on a date by a boy I'd known from our local church. I had liked him since I was five years old. I was very excited that he wanted to go out with me. He wanted to take me to a basketball game at the local public high school. When I asked my dad for permission, he refused. "Why?" I pleaded.

His response was, "There will be people who smoke there and they might influence you to start smoking."

"I'm not going to start smoking. I don't like smoking! We're just going to watch the game! Please let me go!"

His answer to that was, "No!"

There would be no reasonable discussion or boundary that would allow me to prove myself. So I went to my room. I cried out in anger and rage against a father who would control my life without any room for allowing me to prove I was trustworthy. I have never smoked even one time to this day.

There was another situation that further separated me

from my parents emotionally. I had a cousin who was dating a boy of a different ethnicity. He had a brother, Robert, that I thought was kind of cute. I was sixteen at the time. I saw him at church on a weekend leave from the academy. My parents didn't approve of the guy my cousin was dating or his brother. They warned me to have nothing to do with him. There was a belief in the church as well as some cultural prejudice that frowned upon marrying a person of a different ethnicity.

At the end of the school year, I returned home. I went with my family to the eighth grade graduation at our local church school. I knew Robert might show up and realized my parents would be on the watch for the two of us. I understood I couldn't have a relationship with him, but I was troubled that they expected me to act as though he was scum and not even allow for friendly contact. I determined that I would not be rude to him if he should speak to me.

My mother ran the late-as-usual schedule. As we were hurrying to the church for the graduation service, she informed me that I was to wrap the graduation gift at the home of a staff member (who lived by the church school) before going to the reception. I agreed.

After the ceremony, I took the gift and started walking over to the staff member's home. Robert came alongside me as I was walking. Not knowing how to tactfully address my parents' issue with him, I invited him to accompany me. We were granted permission to come inside and wrap the gift. As soon as the gift was wrapped, we left to head over to the social hall, only to realize quickly that my dad was walking towards us with a sullen look on his face. Without a word, Robert left me and I continued walking towards my dad. "You're going to sit with us," he said sternly.

I said nothing. It was pointless. I just followed him. Later, I heard that my mom had pulled up her car behind the car my cousin and her boyfriend were sitting in. She got out and demanded that they tell her where we were, threatening not to leave until they had. I additionally heard that my parents had gone looking for us in an adjacent orchard. I was mortified. The whole interaction was only a few minutes.

By the time I was in college, I was even more emotionally distant from my parents. After meeting my future husband-to-be, Michael, he asked me a question. "Are you excited about going home for the holiday?"

"Not particularly," I said.

"Why not?" he asked.

"I'm not too close to them."

He was surprised and not sure what that meant. I was usually dutiful, outwardly, but my emotional space was considered off limits to my parents. After my first year of college, I spent my summer in a different city with some relatives. At the end of the second year of college, Michael and I were engaged and planning our fall wedding. I spent the summer in the same city, where Michael also lived, until just before the wedding. A few days before the wedding, my dad said something in a stern and controlling way. I reacted angrily, telling him I was glad I was getting married and wouldn't have to be around him. Afterwards I realized I had hurt him and he had cried.

After Michael and I were married, it was easy to maintain the distance in my relationship with my family. Within a couple of years, Michael and I had our first daughter. Two years later, our second daughter was born. My dad loved the babies and enjoyed them with what little contact we had. We lived only three or four hours away, but we were busy raising two small girls, and earning a livelihood, and we rarely called.

Then in 1980, God opened a new door for us spiritually. I began to hear and learn some things about the teachings of my church that caused me to do a double take. My beliefs were dramatically challenged. I began a serious and diligent study of the teachings of my church and was shocked by what I found. Progressively I searched the Word with new revelations which brought me to a spiritual crossroads. Cautiously I began making different choices from what I had been taught in my spiritual upbringing. The foundation was the same; my faith in Jesus was intact, but interpretations of the Bible were different. There was new faith—new understanding about grace and salvation. My view of Christ's atonement was enriched. What he had done for me had new meaning. Jesus was precious to me. It was scary to be making such changes. I had been taught there was no other church or interpretation of Scripture that was true or safe. To believe otherwise would keep me out of heaven.

I was afraid to let my parents know of this change. So it was not talked about for a while, but things were changing. I was changing. There were others from my background making similar changes. Some began to meet together and study together. It was exciting and scary all at once. When I did bring up the changes in my beliefs with my mother, she told me I was deceived by Satan. No matter what evidence I shared with her in support of my convictions, it made no difference to her. One day she told me that I had rejected everything she had taught me. I tried to assure her that the foundation of following Jesus she had laid was still intact.

In September of 1980 I received a call from my mother. My father had fallen from the old walnut tree and had broken his back. He was paralyzed from the waist down and was in the hospital. My response was limited. Would he be OK? There was no assurance that he would get better, but it wasn't known for sure yet. I made no promise to try to come down. At that time, we were living in a small cabin in the foothills of the Sierras. We didn't have much money and transportation was limited. My emotions were stiff, distant. Now when I think back, I am saddened by my lack of compassion and my inability to respond. I was blinded by my hurt and bitterness.

It would take a work of God's grace to bring about the needed change and healing.

My mother was in her last year of teaching kindergarten in the public school where she had taught for thirty-four years. In spite of where she was lacking, she was a strong woman and committed to overcoming hardships. She faithfully drove the forty miles or so each way to see my father in the hospital after work.

My father spent the first three months in the hospital for rehab. He was taught how to make his own transfers from the bed to the wheelchair, from the wheelchair, then to the toilet and back. He had been diabetic since his mid twenties, but had maintained his sugar level through dietary changes. At the time of his accident, his bodily responses caused his blood sugar to change radically so that he had to take medicine for it. Life would never be the same again. I was able to make one visit to him while he was there.

Finally, my father came home. My dad had struggled with depression in his life. I had been concerned that he might go downhill rapidly with this situation. I was glad to see that he adapted well and was making progress in his emotional and physical response. They changed some things in the house to help him maneuver. My mother continued teaching. She would fix him breakfast in the morning before racing off to the school, a block and a half away, come back to fix his lunch at noon, and not return until after school. Mother told me the doctor had said it wasn't necessary to have in-home care. It seems this was poor advice. My dad had poor circulation as a diabetic and with this added situation circulatory stimulation would have been advantageous. Just having another human being to interact with would have been helpful as well. Erroneously, they placed a piece of plastic under my dad to help him slide easier for movement in the bed. Eventually this caused him to develop bedsores. Finally, he had a fever that wouldn't

204 JOURNEYS TO MOTHER LOVE

quit. He was hospitalized again. The diagnosis was that he had strep, staff, and E.coli—serious infections. He was given the strongest antibiotics to overcome this which also depleted his immune system. Dad began to retain fluids. The bedsores were deep and once the doctor pulled on a piece of gauze that he realized was coming from the other sore. The sores were connected.

During this hospitalization, Michael and I had an opportunity to visit my dad. At this time Dad, in a subtle way, brought up the subject of our spiritual change. First, though, he requested of Michael that he should always take good care of me. Michael gave him his word. Secondly, he asked that we would not reject "God's last prophet" (the one significant in my parents' church). I could hear the pain and concern in his voice. I felt sad for him, but at the same time I knew this subject would require more energy and concern than he could invest.

"Daddy," I said, "this is too much for us to talk about right now. But I want you to know that I am following Jesus, and he will lead me in the right direction." He said no more about it. I hope the Lord comforted him with those simple words.

One morning, in the early hours before rising, I had a dream. Nothing spectacular, just simply a picture in which I saw my grandmother and a younger cousin who had already passed away and my dad, apparently deceased, all lying in a mortuary room. When I awoke, I had the sense that God might be preparing me for Dad's passing. Later in the day, I received a message from my mother saying that she felt my dad's passing was near, and she would come and pick me up so I could visit him.

The next day, Mom picked me up and took me to see Dad at the hospital in my hometown. My emotions were muddled: emotional caution mixed with reserved compassion. But my new place with God was stirring within me, though I had a lot of maturing to do. I brought my Bible with me and sat on a chair in the room near my dad. He opened his eyes and recognized me, but in his weakened state he was very fatigued. "I'm so tired," was all he said.

"That's all right, Daddy. I'll just sit here with you. You can rest."

I read from the Scriptures and prayed, then went outside for a while. Tears welled up in my eyes. I felt grief for my father in such a sad condition and suffering such a great loss. He was only sixty-two years of age. Once, when I had leaned over and kissed him on the forehead, he had told me that it hurt. His skin was puffy from toxins and fluids that were no longer leaving his body properly. I desperately wanted to know God's power in this situation.

Later that evening, family members arrived. We gathered around my dad. Mom had sent Dad's favorite baseball cap with me to the hospital. I showed it to him. "Oh, my cap, my red cap—I wish I could wear it," he said.

Later that night, I tossed and turned. My mind groped in the darkness for faith. "God," I prayed, "I believe that you heal. I want to experience your healing for Dad. What should I do?"

I knew that my mother's pastor and elders had already anointed Dad with oil for healing. I finally relaxed, deciding that in the morning I would ask Mom if she would ask again for the elders to anoint Dad with oil. It was a small step of faith. I knew, at this point, healing would come only as a miracle of God. There was nothing left for the doctors to do.

In the morning, my mother came into the room where I was resting. With a step of humility, I shared my thoughts from the night before and asked if she would agree to ask her pastor for a gathering of prayer and anointing on Dad's behalf. She agreed.

During the afternoon, I spent some time alone with God

and in the Word. I pondered the importance of praying in unity. I asked for the pastor to come by the house for a visit before the appointed time for the prayer gathering. When he arrived, I shared the scriptural thoughts and asked if we could agree to pray that God would either heal Dad or take him from this life quickly so he wouldn't continue suffering as he was. We agreed.

That evening, a small intimate group gathered around Dad for prayer. The pastor explained the prayer request and the focus on praying together in agreement. He moved individually around the room with the question, "Do you agree with this request?" He even asked my dad, who answered, "Yes."

We saw no visible healing that night, but I rested in the comfort of our request being laid before God with faith, in agreement. We all left to retire for the night.

The next afternoon, while waiting at my mom's house, the phone rang. I picked it up and answered, "Hello?"

I heard Mom's voice on the other end, "He's gone."

Mom came and picked me up to take me back over to the hospital. We talked quietly around Dad's body. He obviously was no longer there as we had known him. As Mom talked, she shared the story of what had taken place just before he died.

A nurse had entered Dad's room to attend to him. As she turned to do something, he had spoken to her, thanking her for all the help she and others had given him. He acknowledged that he couldn't have made it without their help. She joked with him a little in response, but hearing a sigh, she turned to look. On that hot August afternoon in 1981, eleven months after his accident, Dad had slipped peacefully and quietly away. In less than twenty-four hours, after our prayer gathering, he had returned to his Creator and Savior. I was twenty-six years old at the time.

At once, Mom's life took a dramatic turn. After thirty-four

years of teaching, she was retired. After thirty-nine years of marriage, she was widowed. After almost a year of taking care of a handicapped man, she was released. What would she do now? Mom was a very strong-minded, independent woman. It wasn't long before she began traveling across the country and back, sightseeing and visiting people. A very social woman, she enjoyed her trip. She busied herself with her usual interests, music and flowers, church, and related social connections. If she missed Dad, she seldom let it show. She never remarried. She said she had married for life. I know she loved Dad, even though they had their troubles and differences, but she seldom talked about him. I didn't really understand why. Maybe this was another evidence of her cloaked emotions—her difficulty in addressing the deeper feelings.

In the pursuit of her interests and ambitions, Mom had not been a good housekeeper. She could be meticulously disciplined in certain of her interests, but just as undisciplined when it came to cleaning. On occasion she would decide to deep clean some part of the house, such as stripping the old wax off the floor and re-waxing or cleaning the venetian blinds and windows—but avoid the dishes or the daily needs of order.

As a child of ten years of age and more, I recall the necessity of my investment to bring the house in order for company. My brother became invested in this process as well, and sometimes my dad. My grandmother had done this for many years too. On behalf of my mother, I have an older cousin who said my mother always kept the house clean in her younger days. My mother was thirty-five years old when I was born and forty at the time my brother came along. I don't have any remembrance of those earlier times.

Through the next twenty-three-plus years, Mom lived alone most of the time. For a while my brother was with her. On occasion she would help someone out, allowing them to stay with her. But Mom's ability to keep up with her home didn't change. Her perspective of planning to do it later never came to an end. After living in the same house for fifty-eight years, there was much that hadn't been done. She had become a hoarder. Along with that we began to suspect that dementia was setting in. All the while, this delayed cleaning was becoming an increasingly insurmountable problem for her. Not only did she hoard, but from her early years of being poor and living through the times of the Great Depression, she never wasted food. Her refrigerator was abhorrent. She saved food, bags, plastic plant pots, packing bubbles, and papers, magazines for future reading, tax papers, wrappings, and you name it! We couldn't stay over for any holiday. It just wasn't practical. You could hardly find a place to sleep or eat or function normally!

In the few preceding years before Mom's transition out of her home, she would hire Michael to do construction work for necessary repairs. He replaced the large driveway, hand dug and poured the perimeter footings for the garage, replaced pipes and plumbing, etc. On numerous occasions, he worked there without me. He had years of expertise clashing with her strong headed opinions, now warped by dementia. It wasn't fun, to say the least. When I did come with him, from Colorado where Michael and I and our three daughters now lived (the last one was born after Dad passed away), it would always be centered on working to make a dent in the mess of things! It wasn't ever about just relaxing and enjoying the time together. Mom would fly out to Colorado to be with us for Christmas every year. Even then, a controlled hug was the most emotion she displayed. There were many unresolved issues stuffed down in my heart, and I was too afraid and unsure of how to approach such issues successfully.

Our girls' relationship with my mom was strained as well. Her approach to sharing or teaching what she believed in was usually presented in a dogmatic or hard-sell manner. She was noted for presenting different beliefs or health dogmas to the girls behind our backs. Again, I felt too uncomfortable to attack the problem head-on. I avoided conflict where I could, except when I felt driven to the point of agitation. Then I might spill out a few brief words.

The irony, though, was in her ability to be complimentary and warm to complete strangers! She would visit the sick in the hospital or in the neighborhood, or the lonely with great compassion, yet seem very indifferent and insensitive to those closest to her. In pondering this, I assumed it was a safe interaction that made her shine! There was nothing to work through, relationally. I could admire her heart to reach out to others in need, but it was frustrating to find it lacking toward me and the family. I don't want to say Mom never showed kindness of heart towards us. She would give a gift on occasion, or bring me some bulbs from her yard to plant in mine. I appreciated those expressions of her love. I too, would purchase or make her gifts that I knew would please her or warm her heart; but the healthy intimacy of interaction between a mother and daughter that one would hope for was so lacking.

Back to the mess in Mom's home: I would try to encourage, prod, motivate, and challenge … whatever I could think of to try to influence her to make progress in overcoming the horrible situation of her home. She would promise she was going to … tomorrow. "I've been too busy, too many interruptions to get anything done. But, I'm going to fly in there and work tomorrow for six hours," she'd claim.

When I'd asked her later if she had gotten anything done, she'd tell me she hadn't had time. "Yeah, right, Mom," I'd think to myself. "What does a woman of eighty-some years have to do, that she wouldn't have time to do a little cleaning?"

I felt annoyed with her unrealistic thinking. Finally, I threatened that we wouldn't come back to her house until she at least had the kitchen cleaned up and had made some progress in the bedroom where we stayed. "I'm going to," she'd say. "You'll see." But it was always the same.

I knew I'd have to come back without anything being accomplished. When we were a little ways out from arriving, I gave Mom another call. "Mom," I said, "we'll be there in a couple of hours. Would you make sure the bed is cleared off before we get there? I'm tired and would like to lie down."

"OK, I will," she said.

But upon our arrival, it was still the same. Nothing had been accomplished. I felt really annoyed and frustrated. "Why couldn't she accomplish this much?" I complained to myself.

Finally, my brother and his wife counseled together with us that we were going to have to intervene. Mom could no longer live like this. We would have to overcome the situation for her, like it or not, and help her transition into a better living situation. The thought was monumental, both emotionally and physically. Through the many years she'd lived in this home, she had collected and hoarded stuff in the house, the attic, the garage, the sheds, and the yard!

We informed Mom that this monumental change was pending. I told her that in May I would make a trip out to start the cleaning in earnest. Mom panicked. She envisioned us throwing out her good stuff! She begged me to give her six months to do it herself. She pleaded that this was only fair! She used to tell me that she was the only one who knew what to do with her stuff. I told her that wasn't entirely true. There were many things that could be sorted and organized by people who had good basic common sense. She could hardly wrap her mind around this concept as having any validity. After we repeated this idea to her many times, she did hire someone here and there to help her, but with many limitations and dictations as to how the sorting and cleaning out should be done. Finally, I stood my ground. I told her she had already been given six months and more to accomplish this, and she hadn't been able to do it. Now we would do it.

Mom told me that she had gotten the house cleaned up and there wouldn't be anything for us to do! We found family members where she could go to visit when we would come to work, so as to avoid the unreasonable conflict of her telling us that we couldn't get rid of things that she wanted to save, like magazines that she was going to read someday, or stuff that hadn't been used in years or decades. So by now the whole situation was rather exaggerated in her mind. I questioned her further and discovered she had gained the sympathy of her friends who had helped her to box up and store or hide the stuff, so that we couldn't go through it. That was it! I was furious, and I let her know it!

She left on the prearranged trip, and my sister-in-law and I arrived to begin the proposed task. Sure enough, when we arrived, everything was in order—on the surface. I began to realize that despite what was hidden for the moment, this had actually turned into a blessing. I knew we would have to deal with the hidden things later, but for now the house was at least pleasant and functional. We would work on the closets, cupboards, and drawers that were stuffed to the hilt! Mom's roses were in bloom. Taking a pair of cutters, I took a few minutes to cut some roses and arrange them on the table. They gave us a focus of beauty and peacefulness in the midst of tedious work, challenging decisions, tired bodies, and frustrating memories. God's grace was good.

My sister-in-law worked beside me for about ten days, and I worked alone a few more days before heading home. I picked Mom up at the airport in the Bay Area. While driving to Sacramento, we made small talk. I wouldn't be with her when she arrived home. Any conversation about the past two weeks was avoided or kept to a minimum. I caught my plane back from Sacramento while she drove the two hours home. When I talked with her on the phone later, her only significant response was that the old linoleum that had been on the pantry shelves had still been useable (I had cleaned and replaced the shelves with paper). The second was a question as to where a specific jar was that she liked to use (a juice jar, totally replaceable). For all the days of work that had been put into this situation, that was it! I was glad that she wasn't angry over anything significant, but disappointed by her perspective.

That was the first of several trips over the next few months that it took to prepare Mom's house for the market. Collectively, I spent three-and-a-half months of my own time after we started this mission to move her out of her home. That doesn't include all the others who worked there as well. On one trip, I remember standing just inside the door with a prayer on my mind, "God, how will I ever overcome all this mess? Where do I start?"

The response that came back was, "One piece at a time. Pick up a piece of paper and make a decision as to what to do with it, and then do it again, and again ... one piece of paper at a time, one thing at a time. I remember on one trip having to spend the first few days just dealing with papers and magazines all over the floor in the bedroom to even make a path around the bed. Clearing off piles of stuff to get into the bed, and clutter and dust on the bookshelf headboard in order to function there while we stayed with her. It was no different than Mom's bedroom, though. She had come to the point of sleeping on the couch regularly.

By the weekend, Mike and I would plan a short trip out of town just to have a mental and physical break from it all. I would haul several bags of papers that I had discarded from the bedroom to the back of the truck so I could dispose of them elsewhere. My intent was to prevent her from going through it all and reclaiming it, while we were gone for the weekend. She soon realized what I was doing and made her protest. I stood my ground, assuring her that I was not throwing out anything of value and would dispose of the material in a reasonable fashion. She wasn't convinced, I'm sure, but made no further protest.

Her kitchen was so out of control, as well as the refrigerator, that it was not possible to function there. In the summertime, we could go to the local park and eat our lunch, but not in the winter. For a while before she had to move, Mom would eat meals with a friend, several blocks away, who had a clean home. Her friend was in her nineties, a very pleasant woman, hard of hearing, but with a sense of humor. We became guests along with Mom, bringing in food to share as well. It wasn't the way things should have been, but Beth was a blessing. She provided a place of sanity in all the chaos and disorder.

While all this cleaning and sorting was going on, we really didn't know just where we should place Mom. We expected to find some kind of a senior facility, but where? Neither my brother nor I wanted to have her live near us. That would require more of us emotionally than either one of us wanted to invest. But God had other plans. He gently but firmly began manipulating my thoughts, like a massage therapist loosening up tight muscles to bring a beneficial release. I began to think how I would feel once Mom would leave this life if I didn't allow the Lord to work in our relationship before that time. The thoughts didn't leave me with a sense of peace. Slowly, the Lord's conviction began to settle in my heart. I knew I needed to invite her to live near me.

My husband's initial response was a strong negative! He didn't want to deal with her either. We continued to talk about it. I explained my conviction and urged him to allow me to follow my heart and the Lord's leading in this. He stopped resisting and I found a nice senior facility for Mom a couple of miles away from our house. Her house went into escrow in December of 2004. When she realized that the end of this struggle was in sight, the relief was apparent. We brought her to Colorado for Christmas, she moved into her new home January 2005. When Mom's personal things arrived from California and everything was situated, her new home was comfortable and pleasant. She adapted well and got involved in the activities. She had already attended a local church over the years when she had visited us, so it was an easy transition to become a regular instead of a guest there. For the most part, a significant transition in her life had come to a peaceful landing. But, now the relational part was about to become airborne!

The roles were reversed significantly! I made the decisions that were necessary regarding medical concerns. My brother handled the finances. My mother wasn't allowed to drive. Little by little, more of these decisions that limited her independence were required. She had lost some of her balance and had taken some falls. She was also diagnosed with dementia. Having been quite independent her entire life, this change was hard for her. I found it challenging to lead in the face of her resistance and frustration. I hated the friction it caused.

Then there were the phone calls—too early in the morning, too late at night over insignificant matters. I felt annoyed and would remind her of appropriate boundaries for when she could call. There were doctors' appointments I needed to take her to. Going without me was generally futile with the dementia problems in the equation. I usually thought of myself as a patient person. Other people thought of me that way, too, but Mom had ways of bringing out my lack of patience. Even if I managed to sound reasonably patient on the outside, I was not feeling patient on the inside!

In September that year, Pat, my mother-in-law, arrived for a visit. That evolved into her becoming Mom's roommate at the senior facility. That had its pros and cons! They had enjoyed each other's company whenever they had opportunity to connect over the years, but being roommates was a whole different affair! At first, they were excited. Then they became like sisters, with love/hate relational dimensions. Neither one of them had a sister, but they were in the experience of it now! Slowly they adjusted and the bond between them strengthened and stabilized.

I now had two that needed doctors' appointments, two that had dementia, two that needed my leadership, and two that called at the wrong times with annoying questions. I had to set not only boundaries for them, but for myself. I needed emotional space. When I took Pat to the doctor, Mom would want to ride along as well. I would tell her I was only going to take one at a time. She didn't like it, it made her sad, but it helped my sanity. Then as I was driving one to the doctor's appointment, she would fill me in on the other's objectionable behavior. I had to be a counselor too. Did I mention I had a life apart from them—daughters, grandchildren, and a husband, as well as my own needs?

My plate was full and overflowing. I had emotional baggage to deal with, and I didn't know how. But God in his gentle way had confronted me. After inviting him to loosen my white-knuckled grip on my bag full of emotions, he took me seriously. God began bringing his thoughts to me in gentle but firm nudges—patiently, but tenaciously! One day, I realized he was giving me the directive that I was to start hugging the moms, as we called them now. Not just once in a while, but whenever I came over and before I left. I wasn't excited about this command. That wasn't in my emotional comfort zone. I hadn't grown up with that kind of emotional expression. Hugs were occasional around my home growing up and rarely happened when we felt offended with each other. So how was I going to respond to this command I knew to be from God?

I found myself responding much as a young child would. When it was time to leave their apartment and go home, I found myself hedging and finding subtle ways to slip out without doing it. But God was serious about this. As soon as I would slip out the door, I would receive a strong check in my spirit: "You didn't hug them!"

"OK, Lord, I'll do it next time."

Sometimes I would manage a hug, before leaving quickly. There was such a battle between my flesh and the spirit. But each time I left without giving them a hug, the check in my spirit would come!

The moms' mental challenges continued in a declining pattern. It became necessary for me to set up dispensers for their medications. More outside help was required to come in to accomplish tasks they couldn't do for themselves. My time was limited. I couldn't be there for all their needs and so it became necessary for a move. By God's grace and provision, an assisted living home was found nearby, and they were able to make the move together. It was an important part of their well being.

One afternoon, after moving them into their new home, I was headed down the front steps toward my car, when like clockwork, once again, I received the inevitable check. "You didn't hug them!"

I stopped on the steps, letting out a sigh, and pondered what my response should be. The thought came to my mind that I could go back inside and tell them I had come back in to give them a hug. But immediately a yell welled up inside of me that wanted to escape out my lips but caught only in my thoughts. "Noooo!" I yelled inwardly. "I would have to humble myself to do that!"

"Loritta, what are you doing, telling God no!?"

But even after chiding myself, I felt too proud to go back and give them hugs. I once again told God I would do it next time. But my pride had been exposed. I knew God and I would have another talk soon!

And we did! Once again, I found myself sitting on the couch with my journal. Poised for writing, I asked God what he wanted to talk about, yet knowing this matter of my pride and "the moms" would be the issue. While I penned my thoughts and his in return, he gently led me in the direction of thought he wanted. I shared how I had a hard time with emotional closeness concerning my mom. I could hardly imagine it ever being different. It had always been this way as far back as I could remember. But God assured me if I would bring my emotions to him, it could be different.

"Really?" I questioned.

"Really," he assured me.

After that I became regular about giving hugs. Lots of things were still challenging, but I was being changed. Sometimes I struggled with the fact that since Mom had dementia, in addition to her way of handling things, it was quite likely she was not going to change. It would be only me who changed. One day the phone rang. It was Mom. She began sharing that she knew something was wrong. She shared that she felt I was upset, but she didn't know what to do about it. She asked if I could tell her what she needed to do. I was amazed and surprised to hear her say these words. I was unprepared to give an adequate answer. I struggled a little in trying to find a response, but tried to assure her if I thought of something she could do I would let her know. I then realized that God was allowing me to see that even with dementia he could move on Mom's heart and that I should trust him in this journey.

God was revealing a number of truths to me during this time that applied to my relationship with Mom. One morning I was with a friend who was experienced in natural health remedies. I brought her some items related to natural health that Mom no longer needed, and inquired to see if she could use them. As we talked, she mentioned how my mom was informed in these matters beyond the average person of her time. As she complimented her, I squirmed inside. I felt uncomfortable speaking of my mom in a positive manner.

After all, she had a lot of problems that had caused me and others of our family a lot of pain.

After leaving, I pondered the discomfort I had experienced in that situation. Why did I feel that way? As I reflected more on this matter, I realized that I felt threatened by someone viewing my mom in a positive manner, because I felt that my hurts and wounds from Mom's negative words and attitudes were somehow being negated. If others didn't know how poorly she had treated me, the validity of my pain would be discredited. Yet, I was also convicted that I was in the wrong for only wanting her to be seen as a bad person.

One day the Holy Spirit drew my attention to these verses:

> "[Let your] love be sincere—a real thing: hate what is evil [loathe all ungodliness, turn in horror from wickedness], but hold fast to that which is good. Love one another with brotherly affection—as members of one family—giving precedence and showing honor to one another" (Romans 12:9-10, AMPLIFIED).

As I studied this passage I decided to call it the Love Sandwich. The beginning and the ending were about loving people. I called this the bread. But the meat in the middle caught me by surprise. It used strong emotional words: hate, loathe, and abhor; evil, wickedness, and all ungodliness; hold fast to that which is good. I began to see that God was not negating my pain, but he didn't want me stuck in it! I could hate the wrong done to me, but I was to hold fast to the command that God gave me to love people! I needed to be for the person but against the wrong attitudes and actions. This brought light and new freedom into the picture!

God was drawing me into a deeper walk with him, freeing me from the bondages of sin, even emotional sins, to follow him ... follow his example.

"Consequently, from now on we estimate and regard no
one from a [purely] human point of view—in terms of
natural standards of value. It was God (personally present)
in Christ, reconciling and restoring the world to favor with
Himself, not counting up and holding against [men] their
trespasses [but cancelling them], and committing to us the
message of reconciliation of the restoration to favor" (2
Corinthians 5:16, 19, AMPLIFIED).

How could I cling to my hurts and frustrations in relationship to my mom in light of God's grace to me? My heart was
softening. My fingers were loosening.

After I became obedient to God about hugging the moms,
he gave me another assignment. He let me know I needed to
tell them, "I love you."

That made me squirm! But God had gained territory in
my heart by now. I knew it wasn't about my emotional level
or feelings. It was about obedience. It was about the choice to
love. I moved into this assignment more easily than the first. It
was still challenging. Many times I left hurriedly after a quick
"I love you." But the walls were coming down.

"Let not sin therefore rule as king in your mortal (short-
lived, perishable) bodies, to make you yield to its cravings
and be subject to its lusts and evil passions. Do not continue
offering or yielding your bodily members [and faculties]
to sin as instruments (tools) of wickedness. But offer and
yield yourselves to God as though you have been raised
from the dead to [perpetual] life, and your bodily members
[and faculties] to God, presenting them as implements of
righteousness" (Romans 6:12-13, AMPLIFIED).

Let me paraphrase this for you the way the Holy Spirit
brought it to my attention:

"Don't let your emotions rule as king—to make you give in
to their dictations. Don't continue yielding your emotions to

sin as tools of ungodliness, but offer your emotions to
God—presenting them as implements of righteousness"
(AMPLIFIED).

Wow! This opened a window of freedom! My mind and
my emotions are part of my body, right? So, it was applicable.
You mean my emotions don't "just happen and I can't help it"?
You mean I can take charge and not let them be in control?
Truly his Word was a light unto my path!

One morning as I sat in the Lord's presence, studying his
Word, God dropped another thought in my mind about a new
assignment. This time, the words were, "Feed my sheep."

"OK, Lord," I said. "I know that I'm feeding or helping the
moms with their physical needs—"

But did he mean more than that? Somehow I felt it was
more, but I was hesitant. Though I sensed it meant spiritual
feeding, I put it on the back burner. But God isn't put off easily.
He stirred my mind back to that command numerous times
over the following months. Finally, it weighed on my mind
again. This time I knew I needed to act on it. The Lord had
been bringing the thought to my mind that I could feed his
sheep simply by going to their home and playing the piano,
singing gospel songs with them, and sharing in the Word
together.

One afternoon, I was heading back with my mother-in-
law from a doctor's appointment thinking about this admoni-
tion. I brought up the subject, saying, "I'm going to come
over on Friday and play some gospel songs that we can sing
together. Then we can share in the Word together a little bit."

"OK," she said. "That would be good. We'd like that."

When we met that Friday, a door of blessing was opened.
I sat at the piano while Mom sat in a chair to my right and
Pat sat to my left. As we worshipped the Lord together, the
conflict and struggles were put aside and we were in unity. You

know, it is said that the ground is level at the foot of the cross. And so it was. As we came before the Lord together, we all needed grace for our lives. It was good. It blessed them and it blessed me. They expressed their appreciation time and time again. I could see joy on my mother's face, and love—love and admiration for me, her daughter!

We continued meeting together like this over the next couple of months. One afternoon, I received a call that Mom wasn't feeling well. Within an hour, she was in the hospital. As I drove there, I put my trust in God to take care of her. When I arrived, the attending physician informed me that an MRI had already been done, and she was bleeding into the brain. The diagnosis wasn't good. In a short time, she was comatose. As I looked to the Lord and pondered in my heart as to whether I should intercede for her physical breakthrough or accept this as her time to go, my heart settled on the latter.

Knowing that she might still be able to hear me, I began to talk to Mom. I shared words from the twenty-third Psalm with her. I spoke words that I hadn't yet spoken about forgiving her for hurting me. I told her that if this was her time to go, that I was releasing her to the Lord. Other than speaking with staff and calling family members, I was by her side most of the time, holding her hand.

That evening, the local family members gathered around her bed, from the youngest to the oldest. She couldn't respond, but we spoke to her and stroked her hair. We sang together and prayed together. Finally everyone went home, but me. A bed was placed beside hers for me. My eldest daughter, Laura, brought my Bible and a hymnbook before leaving. I had requested of the Lord many times that when it was Mom's time to go, he would allow me to be with her. And in his goodness, he had answered my prayer. Just after 3:00 a.m. the next morning, September 18, 2008, the Lord took her home. She was eighty-nine.

I sat alone in the room with her body and sang hymns of faith and grace and was comforted. A nurse read to me from my Bible and listened while I shared stories. I appreciated her graciousness.

I reflect now on the goodness and grace of God. I will ever be grateful for his tenacity and mercy to call me out of the bondage of my white-knuckled emotions and show me how to start down the path of healing with him in relationship to my mom. Was everything fixed and perfect when she died? No, but in the presence of Christ, only truth prevails. It will be complete there, "in a moment, in the twinkling of an eye."

I am glad that God granted us those last few joyful weeks of being in Christ's presence together. I will always remember the sweet memory of my mom's face as we sang the songs of the Lord. How sad it would have been if I had not followed the Lord—even if a bit slowly at times. Despite the difficulties, I'm glad I said "yes." It's been a little more than three years now since Mom's passing. The feeding of his sheep is still happening regularly. I still gather with Pat and various others who live where she does, and so the blessing goes on.

And so I hope that you, the reader, will be encouraged to give God permission to loosen your fingers from any "white-knuckled" grip. May you be encouraged to say, "yes." May you experience the joy of finding freedom in any relationship where you've let your emotions rule over your heart and life. God bless you in your journey to love.

> "Remind people ... to ... speak evil of no one, to avoid being contentious, to be forbearing—yielding, gentle, and conciliatory.... For we also were once wasting our days in malice ... and hating one another" (Titus 3:1, 3, AMPLIFIED).

Don't wait. Give God permission now and start your journey to freedom and love.

Loritta was raised in sunny California with one younger brother. She learned early that she had musical and artistic abilities, which she still uses passionately today. Her mother taught her beginning piano lessons and provided art lessons for her at a young age. She also brought her to a personal acceptance of the Lord at the age of five. Loritta attended the early grades in a private parochial school, and then six years of boarding school before college. She and her lifetime mate celebrate their thirty-seventh wedding anniversary this year. They moved to Loveland, Colorado, twenty-one years ago with their three daughters. The girls are grown and married and now there are six grandchildren. Loritta's mother instilled in her a love for flowers and also invested time in helping plant many flowers in the garden Loritta enjoys today.

Loritta loves to share about the faithfulness of the Lord and how God's Word has been the light on her path.

Visit www.JourneysToMotherLove.com
to read blog posts by the contributors of this book,
share the story of your personal journey, and find
helps for healing in mother/daughter relationships.

www.ingramcontent.com/pod-product-compliance
Lightning Source LLC
LaVergne TN
LVHW051047080426
835508LV00019B/1745